The Accidental Vegan

Devra Gartenstein

THE CROSSING PRESS
FREEDOM, CALIFORNIA

For Cintia

Copyright © 2000 by Devra Gartenstein
Cover design by Courtnay Perry
Cover photographs © 1998 Digital Stock
All interior food photographs © 1998 Digital Stock,
    except p. 125 © 1995 PhotoDisc, Inc.
Author photograph by Christine Albright
Interior design by Chitose Baba
Printed in the U.S.A.

For information on bulk purchases or group discounts for this and other Crossing Press titles, please contact our Special Sales Director at 800/777-1048, ext. 203.

Visit our Web site: **www.crossingpress.com**

Library of Congress Cataloging-in-Publication Data
Gartenstein, Devra
    The accidental vegan / by Devra Gartenstein.
        p. cm.
    ISBN 1-58091-079-3 (pbk.)
    1. Vegetarian cookery. 2. Cookery, International. I. Title.
TX837.G322 2000
641.5'636--dc21   00-030706
                                                        CIP

0   9   8   7   6   5   4   3   2

Contents

Preface

Fifteen years ago I found myself with a series of liberal arts degrees and no work. I took a job in a health food store. I liked the people. They were bright and idealistic, working in a domain which, in its small way, helped people live better.

My favorite job was preparing lunch for the staff. I'd have one hour, and an entire store worth of ingredients. The shelves were filled with fascinating items that were new to me, like rice noodles, nori, and umeboshi plums. I played and I learned.

Before long I was preparing my own food and wholesaling it to the store. Eventually I cut out the middleman and started a business which prepares and delivers a week's worth of vegetarian meals directly to people's homes.

From the very beginning my business attracted health-conscious customers. I listened to their concerns and looked for ways to prepare food that was lower in fat and salt but still satisfying. Over time I drew a considerable vegan clientele and saw that the more dairy-free choices I offered, the more food I sold.

After a while I decided to prepare only vegan food. This decision was partly mercenary and partly creative. I learned in junior high school that poets choose to work in haiku and composers confine themselves to the sonata form because constrictions force artists to be nimble and innovative. Because I enjoy dairy myself but have learned to cook without it, my offerings have to be tasty and appealing enough to make me want to eat them.

I am grateful to my customers for teaching me to appreciate foods that can help me live longer and in better health. I am also thankful that they have pointed me toward an endeavor with the potential to help make the world a better place. If more people eat primarily plant-based foods, the earth will be better able to feed its mushrooming population. By reducing our need for meat we can lessen the environmental damage caused by cattle ranching. By eating foods lower in cholesterol and saturated fat we can spare ourselves expensive, complex, and painful medical procedures.

Any cuisine tells the story of its unique time and place. Meals are prepared from the insights and experiences that have touched and changed us. Every time I add a parsnip to a soup stock I thank my late grandmother. When people talk about food I listen. Because techniques, observations, and traditions are handed down through cultures and families, virtually everyone has something to offer. Even people who generally don't cook often have one or two dishes perfected and will tell you about them with pride. I listen to people talking about food in stores and at parties. I eavesdrop shamelessly.

I believe we live in an age in which our individual and collective survival depends on our ability to recognize and change those habits that cannot sustain us in the future. We are confronting the fact that we have depleted many of the earth's resources and destroyed much of her natural beauty. I don't think there is any other period in history where this kind of awareness has worked itself into a generation's collective consciousness. Curbside recycling and token wilderness protection acts probably do little to lessen the magnitude of the problem, but I feel encouraged when I see these small steps. They indicate that we have shifted from the attitude that the earth's bounty is unlimited to the knowledge that much of what we have could soon be gone.

Our generation has an overwhelming responsibility to change behavior patterns that have lasted for millennia. I find our situation fascinating and poignant. I'm glad to have food a concrete entry point since it is so much a part of my everyday life. I don't know whether or not we will destroy this planet or learn to live on it. I do believe that I live a fuller life when I'm convinced that we can make some difference, and in the meantime, I'm enjoying the food.

My cuisine also tells the story of a time in which we have lost much of our connection to the earth but still seek fulfillment through fundamental pleasures. I believe this is an important reason why a large portion of the American population has become considerably more sophisticated about its food choices over the past decade. (You never used to see fresh ginger in mainstream supermarkets.)

We are becoming more aware of the richness of other cultures, and of global interconnectedness. We enjoy a wide range of ethnic restaurants. Vegetarian cuisine in particular draws on the variety of international flavors, and provides alternatives to the meat-based twentieth century American diet, which evolved in the context of a powerful cattle industry and wide open spaces for grazing.

I hope you enjoy these recipes, and adapt them to tell your own stories. We each find our own balance of healthy eating and hedonism, and the people I enjoy most are always shifting this balance, ideally with a sense of humor. In a perfect world our pleasures and our best interests would come together. They occasionally do in this world. In many of these recipes you can use more or less salt or oil or garlic. Find your own balance, and change it often.

Introduction

Minimizing Fat While Maximizing Flavor

Sauté vegetables in stock or water, rather than oil. This can take longer than using oil because water can't reach as high a temperature, but you don't sacrifice much flavor. If you cook vegetables on low heat and cover the pan, you provide heat from both the top and bottom. This speeds up the cooking process and lessens the risk of food sticking to the pan.

Add flavor in every way you can. My mother says, "Always add a little extra of everything." I use fresh herbs whenever they're available and affordable. I also tend to use more salt than the average vegan, but less than the average American. Nothing (except possibly vinegar) brings out flavor the way salt does. In general, when I work with flavorful ingredients with dubious health reputations, I look for a balancing point: how much do I need to add to make this dish tasty? How little can I use and still enjoy the flavor? If you add salt early in the cooking process, you tend to need less to achieve the same amount of flavor. The best salt substitute I've encountered is Bragg's Liquid Aminos. It still has some sodium, but a little bit goes a long way and it tastes like my body needs it.

Practice using timing and attention instead of oil. For example, you can cook pasta without using any oil if you stir it often. If you rinse pasta soon after you drain it, you don't need oil to keep it from sticking together. If you're cooking pasta or grains to mix with other ingredients and you cook them close to the time you'll mix them, then they won't get gummy while they wait. For cold grain salads, rinsing the grains in cold water removes much of the gluten. This makes the grain less sticky so you can use less oil.

It's generally a good idea to measure oil and other high-fat ingredients. I usually cook without measuring, but I find it helpful to introduce a bit of consciousness when I'm working with ingredients I'm trying to use minimally. It keeps me from using more than I need simply because I'm not aware of how much I'm using.

Shopping

I look for opportunities to buy ingredients as close as possible to their point of production. In other words, I try to buy produce directly from farmers, flour right from the mill, and noodles straight from the pasta factory. This ensures their freshness and often results in lower prices because there are fewer middlemen to pay. Even when the prices are comparable, I enjoy the thought that the greatest portion of my dollar is going to the people who have worked the hardest to produce the food.

Fewer middlemen also means that less paper has been pushed and less fossil fuel has been burned in order to get my food to my kitchen.

I find that small ethnic groceries often have better prices and more interesting selections than large chain stores, even when the chain stores pride themselves on having a dazzling array of goods. Of course there are times when there is no substitute for the convenience of a large store where you can shop for both a Thai meal and a Mexican one, but if you have the opportunity and the interest, there is a wealth of stories and surprises at smaller stores. I make a point to ask questions: Which brand of rice noodles do the owners prefer? Where does the produce come from? What does one do with tamarind?

Cooking Well with a Minimum of Time

I think you save more time cooking by planning the steps carefully than by moving quickly. Slower is faster. It's more efficient to cook something slowly than to burn it and have to cook it again and, within reason, it's quicker to stir two smaller batches than one batch that's too large for the bowl.

Of all the ingredients in this book, beans take the most time (but probably the least attention) to prepare. If you're working with a recipe that uses beans, start them well ahead of time. Then prep the veggies in the ways specified in the ingredients list. I've resisted the temptation, when writing out recipes, to lay out every single step because I've observed that it's an important and acquired skill to think ahead and plan a strategy. I figured that these recipes would be more useful if I let you plan some things for yourself, and develop your own systems.

If you're cooking a grain to mix with something else, try to time the grain to finish cooking at the same time the other ingredients are ready. It is much less work to handle grains and pasta when they're just finished than after they've been sitting. Learn to judge quantities by eye whenever possible. That way you don't have to fish around for utensils. With items that are individually assembled, like grape leaves and spring rolls, focus on dishing out the right amount of filling on the first try: attention to this simple step dramatically speeds up time-consuming processes. If you're working with more than one recipe at once, read them together and try to consolidate the steps; for example, chop all the onions or tomatoes together. Many cookbooks tell you how long it takes to prepare an item. I figure that if you're preparing more than one item at once, times will overlap, and the total duration will depend on how well you plan.

Some Thoughts About Recipes

I believe that, at its best, a recipe is a sketch. I am happiest when some-one leaves the quantities behind and simply works with a list of ingredients. I am always surprised and pleased when I give a friend a recipe and the result tastes more like their food than like mine. I enjoy seeing recipes adapted, with new vegetables and different emphases. Every recipe tells a story, and when you choose to do something your own way, you add your own twist to its tale.

Some Thoughts About Ingredients

In various cases I've used brand name products. I do this when a particular product is the best or the only one I know that meets a particular need. For example, Sunspire brand nondairy, barley malt-sweetened chocolate chips are the only sugar-free vegan chocolate chips I've ever encountered. Likewise, Bragg's Liquid Aminos is a relatively unique product that meets a specific need. I hope that, as time goes on, more products like them will become available. In the meantime, I mention them by name because they work best in the recipes in which they appear.

1
Appetizers

Dips

Roll-Ups

Other Finger Foods

Hummus

In my experience, tahini prepared and designed for a Middle Eastern market tastes better and blends more easily with other ingredients than tahini designed for a natural foods market. Middle-Eastern tahini is light and creamy. Natural foods tahini often looks and tastes too much like peanut butter. Sahadi and Joyva are my favorite widely available brands but, in general, if it has Arabic writing on the label or is made somewhere in the Middle East, it's a good bet.

Serve hummus with raw veggies, crackers, tortilla chips, or pita bread. Hummus is one of the world's great dips. I prefer to keep mine really simple. It has all it needs.

1 CLOVE GARLIC

1–2 TABLESPOONS OLIVE OIL

2 CUPS COOKED OR CANNED CHICKPEAS

1 TABLESPOON FRESH PARSLEY

3 TABLESPOONS LEMON JUICE

1/4 CUP TAHINI

1 TEASPOON SEA SALT

1 CUP WATER   ✳ *(Makes 2–3 cups)*

1. Whiz the garlic and olive oil in a food processor.
2. Add the remaining ingredients and process them, slowly adding the water.

Anasazi Bean Dip

These tasty beans are available in natural and specialty food stores.

2 CUPS ANASAZI BEANS

WATER TO COVER

1 ONION, CHOPPED

2 CLOVES GARLIC, MINCED

1 SMALL CAN DICED GREEN CHILES OR 2 FRESH ANAHEIM CHILES, DICED

1 TEASPOON SEA SALT

1 TOMATO, CHOPPED, OR 1 CUP CANNED CRUSHED TOMATOES OR TOMATO PURÉE

1 TABLESPOON CHILI POWDER

1 TEASPOON GROUND CUMIN

1 TEASPOON DRIED OREGANO

2 TABLESPOONS RED WINE VINEGAR   ✳ (Makes 3 cups)

1. Soak the beans for a few hours or overnight.
2. Change the water and cook them in a medium saucepan with all the ingredients except the vinegar for about an hour and a half, until the beans are soft enough to break down when you stir them. Add more water if necessary.
3. Add the vinegar and serve.

Foul Madamas
(Fava Bean Dip)

A cousin of Hummus (page 17) and Babaganoush (page 22). Foul Madamas goes quite well with both of them. Egyptians serve the three dips together in separate mounds on a large plate and call the arrangement "mezze."

2 CLOVES GARLIC, MINCED

1 TABLESPOON CHOPPED FRESH PARSLEY

1 TABLESPOON OLIVE OIL

1 CAN (**14–16** OZ.) FAVA BEANS, DRAINED

1/2 TEASPOON SEA SALT

1 TABLESPOON LEMON JUICE

BLACK PEPPER TO TASTE   ✳ *(Makes 2 cups)*

1. In a small skillet, sauté the garlic and parsley in olive oil for 3–5 minutes.
2. Add the remaining ingredients and heat through, mashing the beans a bit.

Veggie Walnut Paté

This is vaguely reminiscent of chopped liver (in the best way).

1/2 CUP WALNUTS

8–10 BUTTON MUSHROOMS

2 SHALLOTS, CHOPPED

1 CLOVE GARLIC, MINCED

2 CUPS OF A COMBINATION OF ANY OF THE FOLLOWING VEGGIES:

CARROTS

GREEN BEANS

ZUCCHINI

BROCCOLI

CAULIFLOWER

SQUASH (PRECOOKED)

RED OR GREEN PEPPERS

1 TEASPOON DRIED BASIL

1 TEASPOON DRIED MARJORAM

SEA SALT AND BLACK PEPPER TO TASTE

2 TABLESPOONS OLIVE OIL

1 TABLESPOON LEMON JUICE ✳ *(Makes 2–3 cups)*

1. Mix all of the ingredients except the olive oil and lemon juice in a food processor to the consistency of coarse bread crumbs.
2. Heat the olive oil in a small skillet and sauté the mixture for 6–8 minutes.
3. Add the lemon juice and serve.

Babaganoush

Serve this with Hummus (page 17) and pita bread for a light and satis-fying meal.

2 MEDIUM EGGPLANTS

1/4 CUP TAHINI

1 TABLESPOON FRESH PARSLEY

2 TABLESPOONS LEMON JUICE

1 TABLESPOON OLIVE OIL

1 TEASPOON SEA SALT

1/2 TEASPOON BLACK PEPPER

2 CLOVES GARLIC, MINCED   ✳ *(Makes 2 cups)*

1. Preheat the oven to 400 degrees.
2. Poke the eggplants all over with a fork or knife, then roast them on a baking pan until they're wrinkled and soft, about one hour.
3. When they're cool enough to handle, scoop out the pulp and purée it in a food processor or blender with the other ingredients.

Afghani Eggplant Dip

Afghanistan lies between the Middle East and India, and the food tastes like a crossroads cuisine bringing together two of my favorite sets of flavors.

2 MEDIUM EGGPLANTS

10 SPRIGS PARSLEY

2 CLOVES GARLIC, MINCED

3 TABLESPOONS CHOPPED FRESH MINT

2 TABLESPOONS LEMON JUICE

1/2 TEASPOON DRIED DILL

1/2 TEASPOON GROUND CUMIN

1/4 TEASPOON GROUND CARDAMOM   ✳ *(Makes 2 cups)*

1. Preheat the oven to 400 degrees.
2. Poke holes in the eggplant and bake on a cookie sheet until it droops, about one hour.
3. When it is cool enough to handle, remove the skin and purée the flesh with the remaining ingredients in a food processor or blender.

Artichoke Dip

This one is so flavorful it's hard to believe it doesn't harden your arteries. Blend all the ingredients in a food processor or blender.

1 CAN (ABOUT 14 OZ.) ARTICHOKE HEARTS, DRAINED

1/2 POUND TOFU, SOFT OR FIRM

2 TABLESPOONS CHOPPED FRESH BASIL

1 TABLESPOON LEMON JUICE

1 TABLESPOON OLIVE OIL

SEA SALT TO TASTE   ✳(Makes 2 cups)

Basil Mayonnaise

I've been caught, on occasion, eating this dip with a spoon. Serve it with Deep-Fried Artichoke Hearts (page 39). Mix all the ingredients.

1 CUP SAFFLOWER MAYONNAISE

2 TABLESPOONS CHOPPED FRESH BASIL

1 CLOVE GARLIC, MINCED   ✳ (Makes 1 cup)

Roasted Pepper Dip

I made this dip once for a party I catered, and one woman followed me around all evening saying, "It's like life! This dip tastes like life!" Purée all the ingredients in a food processor or blender.

1 JAR (AT LEAST **8** OZ.) ROASTED RED PEPPERS, DRAINED

1 CAN (**14** OZ.) ARTICHOKE HEARTS, DRAINED

1/2 CUP ALMONDS, WHOLE, WITH SKINS

1 CLOVE GARLIC, MINCED

1 TABLESPOON LEMON JUICE

1/2 CUP FRESH BASIL LEAVES   ✳ *(Makes 2 cups)*

Eggrolls

These can be an appetizer or a meal in themselves. They taste a lot like the traditional Chinese ones. You'll know the oil is hot enough when you can toss a drop of water at the surface and it bounces. Serve these with Plum Sauce (page 174), Teriyaki Marinade (page 177), and Chinese hot mustard.

FILLING:

1 ONION, CHOPPED

1 CLOVE GARLIC, MINCED

1 TABLESPOON GRATED GINGER

1 TABLESPOON OLIVE OIL

1 CARROT, GRATED

6–8 MUSHROOMS, MINCED

1 CUP FINELY CHOPPED BOK CHOY OR NAPA CABBAGE

1/2 CUP MUNG BEAN SPROUTS

1 CAN (8 OZ.) SLICED WATER CHESTNUTS, DRAINED AND FINELY CHOPPED

1 CAN (8 OZ.) BAMBOO SHOOTS IN STRIPS, DRAINED

2–3 TABLESPOONS SOY SAUCE

1 TEASPOON TOASTED SESAME OIL

CORN, PEANUT, OR VEGETABLE OIL, ENOUGH TO PUT AN INCH OF OIL IN A MEDIUM SAUCEPAN

1 PACKAGE EGGROLL OR SPRING ROLL WRAPPERS (CHECK THE INGREDIENTS. YOU CAN FIND THE SKINS WITHOUT EGG.)   ✳ *(Makes 15–20)*

1. In a medium saucepan, sauté the onion, garlic, and ginger in olive oil for about 5 minutes. Add the remaining filling ingredients and cook another 10 minutes.
2. Heat the oil slowly in a medium saucepan. Meanwhile, assemble the rolls. Lay a wrapper in front of you diagonally, like a diamond. Place 2–3 tablespoons filling in a horizontal line in the middle, using as little juice as you can. Fold the bottom corner toward the middle, then fold the side corners toward the center. With your finger, spread a bead of water along the remaining edges, the flap of the envelope. Finish rolling from bottom to top, as tightly as you can without ripping the wrapper. Use the wet edges to seal the roll.
3. Fry a few rolls at a time and drain them on paper towels or brown bags.

Potstickers

Think of tortellini, ravioli, pierogi, or kreplach. There's something so satisfying about a savory mixture wrapped in dough.

FILLING INGREDIENTS FOR EGGROLLS (PAGE 26)

1 PACKAGE WONTON OR POTSTICKER WRAPPERS

OIL FOR DEEP FRYING (OPTIONAL)   ✳ *(Makes about 40)*

1. Prepare the filling in the eggroll recipe but chop everything in much
   smaller pieces. (Nothing should be larger than a pea.)
2. Assemble the potstickers by putting a small teaspoon of filling in
   the center of each wrapper, lightly wetting the edges of the top half
   of the wrapper, then folding the wrapper in half and pressing the
   ends together.
3. Either deep fry or steam them. If you steam them, brush a layer of
   vegetable oil on the steamer to keep them from sticking.

Hummus-Roasted-Pepper Roll-Ups

These bite-sized spirals are quick and easy to assemble. They disappear quickly.

6 BIG FLOUR TORTILLAS

1 BATCH HUMMUS (PAGE 17)

1 JAR (8 OZ., MORE OR LESS) ROASTED RED PEPPERS, DRAINED AND CUT INTO THIN STRIPS
✳ *(Makes about 36 bite-sized pieces)*

1. With a spatula, cover a tortilla with a thin layer of hummus.
2. Arrange a small handful of pepper strips, staggering them so that when you roll, they won't all end up in the same piece. Leave 2 inches at each end without peppers.
3. To start rolling, fold about a half inch from left to right. Roll it as tightly as you can without squeezing out the peppers. Slice the roll in bite-sized pieces.

Mu Shu Veggie Rolls

When you order a mu shu plate in a Chinese restaurant, you get a variety of components which you assemble into burrito-like rolls. In this recipe you assemble them ahead of time, and serve them as appetizers.

1/2 POUND FIRM TOFU, CUT IN STRIPS

1 BATCH PLUM SAUCE (PAGE 174)

1/2 ONION, MINCED

1 TABLESPOON GRATED GINGER

2 CLOVES GARLIC, MINCED

1 TABLESPOON OLIVE OIL

1 TABLESPOON SOY SAUCE

3 CARROTS, GRATED

1 BUNCH BABY BOK CHOY, CHOPPED

8–10 FLOUR TORTILLAS, 8-INCH DIAMETER

3 CUPS COOKED BROWN RICE   ✳ (Makes 8–10 rolls)

1. Marinate the tofu in half the plum sauce.
2. In a medium saucepan, sauté the onion, ginger, and garlic in the olive oil and soy sauce for 5 minutes, then add the carrots and bok choy. Cook on medium heat for another 5 minutes.
3. Spread a layer of plum sauce on each tortilla, then spread a heaping tablespoon of rice and 1/2 cup of the veggie mixture. Roll and serve.

Rice Paper Spring Rolls

These grow easy with practice. They're refreshing, crunchy, and summery. Serve with Peanut Sauce (page 176).

1/2 POUND RICE NOODLES

WATER TO COVER

20 LEAVES FRESH BASIL

20 LEAVES FRESH MINT

2 CUPS SALAD GREENS

1/2 POUND FIRM TOFU, CUT IN LONG, THIN STRIPS

1 TABLESPOON GRATED GINGER

1/4 CUP SOY SAUCE

2 TABLESPOONS LIME JUICE

1 PACKAGE RICE PAPER SPRING ROLL WRAPPERS
(AVAILABLE IN **A**SIAN GROCERIES**)**   ✳ *(Makes 15–20 rolls)*

1. Soak the rice noodles in boiling water for 10 minutes, then drain and rinse them with cold water. Add all the remaining filling ingredients and mix well.
2. Prepare a bowl of warm water large enough to dip the spring roll wrappers.
3. Dip six wrappers, one at a time, and spread them on a table in front of you. Put 1/4 cup filling on each wrapper. The wrappers should soften by the time you spoon the filling onto all six.
4. Fold the bottom of the wrapper up over the filling, then fold each side toward the center. Roll from the bottom to the top of each roll, as tightly as you can without ripping the wrapper. If you do rip it, wrap another wrapper around the whole thing when you roll the next batch.

Nori Rolls

A crunchy, flavorful vegetarian sushi. Nori is a seaweed product, pressed into rectangular sheets. The sliced sections make a colorful appetizer tray. You'll need a bamboo sushi mat. They're available in natural foods stores and Asian groceries.

2 TABLESPOONS GRATED GINGER

3 TABLESPOONS RICE VINEGAR

2 CUPS SHORT GRAIN BROWN RICE COOKED IN **4** CUPS WATER

3 TABLESPOONS TAHINI

3 TABLESPOONS SOY SAUCE

10 SHEETS NORI

4 CARROTS, CUT INTO STICKS **3–5** INCHES LONG

20 GREEN BEANS, TRIMMED

3 TABLESPOONS UMEBOSHI
(PICKLED PLUM) PASTE

✳ *(Makes 60–80 bite-sized pieces)*

1. Soak the ginger in the rice vinegar for 15 minutes.
2. Mix the cooked rice with tahini, soy sauce, ginger, and vinegar in a large bowl. Spread it as thinly as possible, then put it in the refrigerator to cool.
3. When the rice mixture is cool, place a sheet of nori horizontally on the sushi mat. Spoon about a half cup of rice mixture onto the sheet and spread it into a thin horizontal layer, starting about an inch from the edge of the nori closest to you. Place 2 carrot sticks and 2 green beans in a horizontal line in the center of the rice. Roll the mat tightly around the nori, using the mat to press the roll together. The mat will end up in the center of the roll. Unroll it and remove the mat, then form the roll again. Seal the roll with about 1/2 teaspoon of umeboshi paste.
4. Cut each roll into 8–12 pieces. This will be easiest if you have a sharp or a serrated knife. Serve with soy sauce, wasabi horseradish, and pickled ginger.

Dolmades
(Stuffed Grape Leaves)

Each Middle Eastern country has its own variety of grape leaf filling.
This is a Greek recipe. Serve it with Tahini Dressing (page 210).

1 ONION, MINCED

1 TABLESPOON OLIVE OIL, DIVIDED

2 CUPS SHORT GRAIN BROWN RICE, COOKED

2 TABLESPOONS TOMATO PASTE

1/2 CUP RAW SUNFLOWER SEEDS

1/2 TEASPOON GROUND CINNAMON

2 TABLESPOONS LEMON JUICE

1/2 TEASPOON SEA SALT

PINCH BLACK PEPPER

1 JAR (**8** OZ.) GRAPE LEAVES, DRAINED

✳ *(Makes 20–30)*

1. In a small saucepan, sauté the onion in half the olive oil, then mix it with the remaining ingredients, except the grape leaves.
2. Preheat the oven to 375 degrees.
3. Spread out 10 grape leaves, with the darker side facing down. Spoon a teaspoon of filling onto each leaf.
4. Fold the bottom up, the sides toward the middle, then roll toward the top. Place them on an oiled pan, then brush the tops with the remaining oil.
5. Bake, covered, for 35–40 minutes.

Stuffed Mushrooms

My mother makes these on special occasions, with butter instead of olive oil. These are a close second. This recipe is most special if you use the largest button mushrooms you can find, and peel them. When you remove the stem from a large mushroom, the skin in the middle will start to peel away from the rest of the mushroom. Use this as your starting point to peel away the rest of the skin.

1 POUND MUSHROOMS

1 ONION, CHOPPED

4–6 TABLESPOONS OLIVE OIL, DIVIDED

1 TEASPOON SEA SALT

1 TEASPOON DRIED BASIL

1 CUP BREAD CRUMBS   ✴ *(Makes 10 large or 20 small mushrooms)*

1. Preheat the oven to 375 degrees.
2. Wash the mushrooms and remove the stems. Finely chop the stems and sauté them, along with the onion, in a small skillet with a few tablespoons of olive oil for about ten minutes. When the mixture is ready it will begin to look wet. Add the sea salt, basil, and bread crumbs.
3. Put about a tablespoon of filling in each mushroom, rounding the top with the spoon.
4. Pour the remaining oil in a baking pan, set the mushrooms carefully in the pan, and bake for 45–55 minutes.

Deep-Fried Artichoke Hearts

Okay, they're indulgent, but once or twice a year maybe? Serve them with Basil Mayonnaise (page 24).

2–3 CUPS CORN OR VEGETABLE OIL

1/2 CUP FLOUR

1/2 TEASPOON SEA SALT

1 CAN QUARTERED ARTICHOKE HEARTS, DRAINED   ✳ *(Makes 15–20)*

1. Heat the oil in a small skillet on a medium flame. You'll know the oil is hot enough when you can fling a drop of water into the pot and it bounces off the surface.
2. Mix the flour and the sea salt.
3. Toss the artichoke hearts with the flour mixture.
4. Add the artichoke hearts one at a time, waiting about 30 seconds between them. Use tongs.
5. When the artichokes start to brown, take them out of the oil and drain them on paper towels or brown bags.

Rice Balls with Umeboshi Plums

These rice balls are tasty and filling, with a surprise at the center. They keep well and make an excellent snack to take along on a hike or bicycle ride. Watch for pits when you eat them!

3 CUPS COOKED SHORT GRAIN BROWN RICE

1 TABLESPOON TAHINI

2 TABLESPOONS SOY SAUCE

1 TEASPOON GRATED GINGER

1 TABLESPOON RICE VINEGAR

6 UMEBOSHI PLUMS (AVAILABLE IN NATURAL FOODS STORES)

1/4 CUP BLACK SESAME SEEDS
(AVAILABLE IN ASIAN GROCERIES)   ✳ *(Makes 6 balls)*

1. Mix all the ingredients except the plums and the sesame seeds.
2. Shape balls (a little larger than golf balls) with your hands, wetting your fingers if rice sticks to them.
3. Press a plum in the center of each ball, then roll them in sesame seeds.

2
Soups

Veggie Stock

There is no question that the best soups start with lovingly prepared stock that simmers for hours. On the other hand, it's been my experience that you can usually make a tasty, easy soup without fussing over the stock. If you don't have the time to prepare stock in advance, you can start with water and add a parsnip to the broth you're preparing, then pull it out at the end. You can use a couple of strips of kombu, or kelp (available in natural food stores), in the same way.

4–6 QUARTS WATER

1 CARROT

1 ONION

1 POTATO

1 PARSNIP

2 CLOVES GARLIC

1 TABLESPOON SEA SALT

1 TEASPOON BLACK PEPPER   ❊ *(Makes 3–4 quarts)*

1. Combine all the ingredients and cook in a medium stockpot, uncovered, for 1–2 hours.
2. Drain the stock and discard the veggies.

Quick Tomato Soup

You can make this soup in 15–20 minutes if you have the rice on hand.

1 ONION, CHOPPED

1 STALK CELERY, CHOPPED

1 TABLESPOON OLIVE OIL

1 CAN (ABOUT **48** OZ.) TOMATO JUICE

1 CUP FROZEN PEAS

1 TEASPOON SEA SALT

1/2 TEASPOON BLACK PEPPER

1 TEASPOON DRIED DILL

1 CUP COOKED BROWN RICE   ✳ *(Makes 4–6 servings)*

1. In a medium stockpot, sauté the onion and celery in olive oil for about 5 minutes.
2. Add the remaining ingredients except the rice, and cook another 15–20 minutes.
3. Add the rice, heat it through, and serve.

Thai Tomato Soup

Creamy, tangy, and simple. Serve it with Spinach and Tofu in Peanut Sauce (page 101) or Thai Curry with Seitan (page 134).

1 TABLESPOON GRATED GINGER

2 CUPS CHOPPED BOK CHOY

1/4 CUP CHOPPED FRESH BASIL LEAVES

2 CUPS STOCK OR WATER

1 CAN (**48** OZ., MORE OR LESS) TOMATO JUICE

3–4 TABLESPOONS SOY SAUCE

1 CUP BEAN SPROUTS

1/2 CUP COCONUT MILK

2 TABLESPOONS LIME JUICE   ✳ *(Makes 6–8 servings)*

1. Cook the ginger, bok choy, and basil in the stock or water in a medium stockpot for 10 minutes.
2. Add the tomato juice, soy sauce, and bean sprouts and cook another 10 minutes.
3. Add the coconut milk and lime juice and serv

Mexican Tomato Soup

Add Tabasco to make this one hotter, if you'd like.

2 CLOVES GARLIC, MINCED

2 TABLESPOONS CHOPPED CILANTRO

1 TABLESPOON OLIVE OIL

1 CAN **(48** OZ.) TOMATO JUICE

1 CUP FROZEN CORN

1 SMALL CAN DICED GREEN CHILES, DRAINED

1 TEASPOON SEA SALT

1–2 TABLESPOONS LIME JUICE

CRUSHED TORTILLA CHIPS FOR GARNISH

✳ *(Makes 6 servings)*

1. In a medium stockpot, sauté the garlic and cilantro in olive oil.
2. Add the remaining ingredients, except the tortilla chips. Cook on medium heat for 15–20 minutes, then serve topped with tortilla chips.

Gazpacho

This is a perfect summer soup, with no fat.

4 TOMATOES (IDEALLY RIPE, IN SEASON)

1 CUCUMBER, PEELED AND CUT IN CHUNKS

2 TABLESPOONS CHOPPED FRESH TARRAGON

2 TABLESPOONS CHOPPED FRESH BASIL

2 TABLESPOONS RED WINE VINEGAR

1 TEASPOON SEA SALT

2 CUPS TOMATO JUICE

TABASCO TO TASTE   ✳ *(Makes 4–6 servings)*

1. Purée all the ingredients except the tomato juice and Tabasco in a food processor or blender.
2. Transfer to a bowl and whisk in the remaining ingredients.

Miso-Noodle Soup

This is a hearty, strange, satisfying soup. When I first tasted it I was a bit unsettled by the kombu, but now I pick out the chewy pieces and eat them first. I like to make a big pot of this soup when I'm sick, or after a holiday like Halloween or New Year's, when I'm prone to overindulge. The kombu is available in natural foods stores.

1 PACKAGE KOMBU (KELP)

3 QUARTS VEGGIE STOCK, DIVIDED

1 ONION, CHOPPED

2 TABLESPOONS GRATED GINGER

3 CARROTS, SLICED

1/2 CUP SOY SAUCE

1/2 POUND FROZEN PEAS

1 POUND FIRM TOFU, CUT IN SMALL CUBES

1/2 POUND RICE NOODLES

3 TABLESPOONS MISO (ANY KIND)

3 TABLESPOONS RICE VINEGAR   ✳ *(Makes 8–10 servings)*

1. Soak the kombu in enough stock to cover it. When it softens, cut it into bite-sized pieces. Save the stock and add it to the soup later.
2. In a medium stockpot, sauté the onion and ginger in one cup of stock until the onion is tender.
3. Add all the remaining stock, carrots, and kombu pieces. Bring to a boil and simmer for 5–10 minutes, then add the soy sauce, peas, and tofu, and simmer another 5 minutes.
4. Turn off the heat and add the rice noodles. Skim off a cup of stock, dissolve the miso in it, then add this to the soup along with the rice vinegar.
5. Let it stand, covered, about 10 minutes, until the rice noodles are soft, then serve.

Hot and Sour Soup

This soup has a wonderful variety of flavors and textures. Serve it with Lo Mein (page 68), or Chinese Veggies with Black Bean Sauce (page 104).

6–8 CUPS VEGGIE STOCK

1 MEDIUM ONION, CHOPPED

2–3 CLOVES GARLIC, MINCED

2 TABLESPOONS GRATED GINGER

10 MUSHROOMS, CHOPPED (BUTTON, SHITAKE, OYSTER— A VARIETY WORKS WELL)

2 CARROTS, CUT IN THIN STRIPS

1/4 POUND FIRM TOFU, CUT IN STRIPS

1 SMALL CAN BAMBOO SHOOT STRIPS, DRAINED

1 SMALL CAN SLICED WATER CHESTNUTS, DRAINED AND FINELY CHOPPED

1/2 CUP PEAS, FRESH OR FROZEN

4 TABLESPOONS SOY SAUCE (MORE OR LESS, TO TASTE)

3 TABLESPOONS RICE VINEGAR

1 TABLESPOON TOASTED SESAME OIL

1 TEASPOON–**1** TABLESPOON CHILE OIL (AVAILABLE IN ASIAN GROCERIES)

✳ *(Makes 6–8 servings)*

1. In a medium stockpot, bring the stock to a boil and add the onions, garlic, ginger, mushrooms, and carrots. Boil, covered, for 30–40 minutes.
2. Add the remaining ingredients except the sesame and chile oils, and cook another 5–10 minutes.
3. Add the sesame and chile oils and serve.

Hot and Sour Soup with Lemongrass

Take the extra time to find the lemongrass and lime leaves. It's worth the effort. They're available in Asian groceries and exemplary super-markets.

2 STALKS CHOPPED FRESH LEMONGRASS (CHOP FAIRLY LARGE PIECES, SO YOU CAN PICK THEM OUT LATER.)

6–8 LIME (OR KAFIR) LEAVES

1 ONION, CHOPPED

1 TABLESPOON GRATED GINGER

2 CLOVES GARLIC, CHOPPED

2 RIPE TOMATOES, CHOPPED

10–12 MUSHROOMS, QUARTERED

6–8 CUPS VEGGIE STOCK

2 TABLESPOONS CHOPPED FRESH BASIL

2 TABLESPOONS CHOPPED FRESH MINT

1/2 CUP COCONUT MILK

3–4 TABLESPOONS SOY SAUCE

1 TABLESPOON RAW SUGAR (OPTIONAL)

2–3 TABLESPOONS LIME JUICE

CHILE OIL TO TASTE

✳ (Makes 6 servings)

1. In a medium stockpot, boil the lemongrass, lime leaves, onion, ginger, garlic, tomato, and mushrooms in the stock for 30 minutes.
2. Add the remaining ingredients except the lime juice and chile oil and cook another 10–15 minutes.
3. Add the lime juice and chile oil, pick out the lemon grass and lime leaves, and serve.

Split Pea Soup

If you add a bit of liquid smoke or tofu hot dogs to this soup, it can really remind you of the carnivorous version.

1 POUND DRIED SPLIT PEAS

2–3 QUARTS VEGGIE STOCK

SEA SALT AND BLACK PEPPER TO TASTE

1 ONION, CHOPPED

3–6 CLOVES GARLIC, MINCED

2 CARROTS, CHOPPED

2 RED OR YUKON GOLD POTATOES, PEELS ON, CHOPPED

1 TABLESPOON POWDERED MUSTARD

1 SMALL CAN TOMATO SAUCE

1 TEASPOON DRIED DILL ✳ *(Makes 6–8 servings)*

1. Sift through the split peas for rocks, then boil them in the stock with sea salt and black pepper. Use a medium stockpot.
2. After 30 minutes add the onion, garlic, carrots, and potatoes. Cook for another 30 minutes.
3. Add the mustard, tomato sauce, and dill, and cook for another 10 minutes.

Dahl
(Curried Lentil Soup)

You can use this as a sauce for rice or a curry, like Dev's Basic Curry (page 84) or you can eat it with a spoon, like soup. It's thick and satisfying, like split pea soup. You can substitute 1 tablespoon curry powder for the four spices if you wish.

4 CUPS WATER

1 CUP RED LENTILS OR YELLOW SPLIT PEAS

1 TABLESPOON GRATED GINGER

2 CLOVES GARLIC, MINCED

1 TEASPOON GROUND CUMIN

1/2 TEASPOON GROUND CORIANDER

1/2 TEASPOON GROUND TURMERIC

1/2 TEASPOON GROUND CARDAMOM

1 TEASPOON SEA SALT

2 TABLESPOONS LEMON JUICE (OPTIONAL)   ✳ *(Makes 6 servings)*

1. Boil the water in a small stockpot and add all the ingredients except the lemon juice.
2. Cook on low heat, stirring often, for about 45 minutes.
3. Add the lemon juice, if desired, stir, and serve.

Greek Lentil Soup

As far as I'm concerned, you can never make too many different kinds of lentil soup. I enjoy this one with Greek Lasagna (page 80) or Spanakopita (page 98).

2 CUPS LENTILS

6–8 CUPS STOCK OR WATER

1 ONION, CHOPPED

3 CLOVES GARLIC, MINCED

1/2 TEASPOON GROUND CINNAMON

1 TEASPOON DRIED DILL

1 TEASPOON SEA SALT

1 TOMATO, CHOPPED

2 CARROTS, CHOPPED

2 TABLESPOONS LEMON JUICE   ✳ *(Makes 6 servings)*

1. Cook the lentils in the stock in a medium stockpot with the onion, garlic, and seasonings.
2. After 20 minutes add the tomato and chopped carrots.
3. Cook for another 20–30 minutes on medium low heat, stirring often.
4. Add the lemon juice just before serving.

Egyptian Lentil Soup

Serve this soup with Dolmades (page 36). The mint gives it a lighter flavor than most lentil soups. You can add some kale or red bell pepper if you like.

2 CUPS LENTILS

8 CUPS VEGGIE STOCK OR WATER

2 TOMATOES

2 CARROTS, CHOPPED

1 ONION, CHOPPED

2 CLOVES GARLIC, MINCED

1 TEASPOON GROUND CUMIN

1 TEASPOON DRIED SPEARMINT

1 BUNCH MUSTARD GREENS, CHOPPED

1 TABLESPOON LEMON JUICE   ✳ *(Makes 6 servings)*

1. In a medium stockpot, boil the lentils in the water or stock with all the ingredients except the mustard greens and lemon juice.
2. Cook, uncovered, for 30–40 minutes, then add the mustard greens and cook another 20 minutes. Add more water as needed.
3. When the greens and lentils are soft, add the lemon juice and serve.

Borscht

This soup is an amazing color and high in iron.

6 MEDIUM BEETS

WATER TO COVER

4–6 CUPS VEGGIE STOCK OR WATER

2 PARSNIPS, PEELED AND CUT IN CHUNKS

2 CARROTS, CUT IN CHUNKS

1 ONION, QUARTERED

2 CLOVES GARLIC

1 POTATO, QUARTERED

1 CUP SHREDDED CABBAGE

1 BUNCH FRESH DILL (YOU CAN USE DRIED DILL, BUT THEN IT WON'T TASTE OR SMELL QUITE LIKE MY GRANDMOTHER'S BORSCHT.)

1 TEASPOON SEA SALT

1/2 TEASPOON BLACK PEPPER

2 TABLESPOONS WHITE, DISTILLED VINEGAR   * *(Makes 6 servings)*

1. Take the tops off the beets and boil them whole in enough water to cover them. Use a medium pot. Cook them for about 45 minutes.
2. In a separate stockpot, boil the veggie stock with all the other ingredients except the vinegar for about 45 minutes.
3. Using tongs, take one beet out of the pot, run cold water on it, and see if you can rub off the skin with your fingers. If you can, drain the beets and peel them this way. If you can't, put it back and cook it until you can.
4. When the other veggies are done, drain the broth and keep it aside.
5. Blend the cooked veggies (including the beets) in a food processor or blender. Add a little stock if they don't blend smoothly. Whisk them together with the broth and vinegar, and serve.

Mushroom Barley Soup

The seasonings in this soup remind me of the Russian-Polish-Jewish food my ancestors ate.

4–6 CUPS VEGGIE STOCK OR WATER

1/2 POUND MUSHROOMS, SLICED

1/2 CUP BARLEY

3 CARROTS, SLICED

2 PARSNIPS, SLICED

1 ONION, CHOPPED

2 CLOVES GARLIC, MINCED

1 TABLESPOON DRIED DILL

1–2 TEASPOONS SEA SALT

1/2 TEASPOON BLACK PEPPER   ✳ *(Makes 6 servings)*

1. Bring the stock to a boil in a medium stockpot.
2. Add the other ingredients and simmer, covered, for 45 minutes to an hour, until the barley is soft.

Potato-Leek Soup

Here's a simple, low-fat version of a tasty, traditional soup.

6 CUPS VEGGIE STOCK OR WATER

4 MEDIUM POTATOES, QUARTERED, UNPEELED

3 LEEKS, CUT LENGTHWISE, CLEANED, THEN CUT IN CHUNKS

2 CLOVES GARLIC, MINCED

2 TABLESPOONS CHOPPED PARSLEY

1 TEASPOON DRIED DILL

1 TEASPOON SEA SALT

1/2 TEASPOON BLACK PEPPER

1 TABLESPOON LEMON JUICE (OPTIONAL)   ✳ *(Makes 6 servings)*

1. In a medium stockpot, boil all of the ingredients in the stock except the lemon juice. Cook for 30–40 minutes, until the potato is soft.
2. Strain the veggies, reserve the stock, then purée the veggies and whisk them back into the stock.
3. Add the lemon juice, if desired, and serve.

Curried Peanut Butter Soup

1 ONION, CHOPPED

1 TABLESPOON GRATED GINGER

2 CLOVES GARLIC, MINCED

2 TOMATOES, CHOPPED

6–8 MUSHROOMS, QUARTERED

1 TEASPOON GROUND CUMIN

1/2 TEASPOON GROUND CORIANDER

1/2 TEASPOON GROUND CARDAMOM

CAYENNE TO TASTE

1–2 TEASPOONS SEA SALT

6–8 CUPS STOCK OR WATER

1 ZUCCHINI, CHOPPED

1 BUNCH COLLARD GREENS, CLEANED, TRIMMED, AND CHOPPED

1 CUP PEANUT BUTTER, CHUNKY OR SMOOTH

2–3 TABLESPOONS LIME JUICE   ✳ *(Makes 6 servings)*

1. In a medium stockpot, boil the onion, ginger, garlic, tomatoes, mushrooms, spices, and sea salt in the stock for about 30 minutes.
2. Add the zucchini and collard greens and cook another 10–15 minutes.
3. Remove a cup of the soup and mix it with the peanut butter and lime. Blend this mixture with the rest of the soup and serve.

Potato Corn Chowder

Mashing the potatoes makes this soup creamy, not unlike a traditional chowder.

6 CUPS VEGGIE STOCK OR WATER

2 POUNDS POTATOES, NOT PEELED, CHOPPED

1 ONION, CHOPPED

2 CLOVES GARLIC, MINCED

1 TOMATO, CHOPPED

1 TEASPOON DRIED BASIL

1 TEASPOON DRIED MARJORAM

1 TEASPOON DRIED THYME

1 TEASPOON SEA SALT

1/2 TEASPOON BLACK PEPPER

1 CUP FROZEN CORN   ✳ *(Makes 6 servings)*

1. In a medium stockpot, cook the potatoes in the stock or water for 30–40 minutes, along with the onion, garlic, tomato, spices, sea salt, and black pepper.
2. Take out 2 cups of cooked potatoes (use tongs or a slatted large spoon), mash them, then add them back to the stock.
3. Mix well, add the corn, and cook for another 5–10 minutes.

Curried Squash Soup

This is a comforting winter soup, thick enough to be filling, but surprisingly light from the ginger and lemon flavors.

2 ACORN SQUASH

2 CARROTS, CUT IN CHUNKS

1 ONION, PEELED AND QUARTERED

1 PARSNIP, CUT IN CHUNKS

1 TABLESPOON GRATED GINGER

1/2 TEASPOON GROUND CARDAMOM

4 CUPS VEGGIE STOCK OR WATER

1 TEASPOON SEA SALT

1 TABLESPOON LEMON JUICE ✳ *(Makes 6 servings)*

1. Cut the squash in half and remove the seeds. Steam for 20–30 minutes, until it's soft.
2. Boil all the remaining ingredients except the lemon juice in the stock.
3. When the squash is ready, scoop out the flesh and cook it with the remaining ingredients for about 15 minutes.
4. Drain the veggies and reserve the liquid. Purée the veggies and mix them with the liquid and lemon juice.

3
Main
Dishes

Pasta Dishes

Curries

Mexicana

Miscellaneous

Pasta Primavera

Pasta and herbs, with veggies you haven't tasted since last spring.

2 QUARTS WATER

1 RED ONION, CHOPPED

2 CLOVES GARLIC, MINCED

1 TABLESPOON OLIVE OIL

1/2 CUP WHITE WINE

3 TABLESPOONS CHOPPED FRESH BASIL

1 TEASPOON SEA SALT

1 BUNCH ASPARAGUS, TRIMMED AND CUT IN BITE-SIZED PIECES

1 RED BELL PEPPER, SEEDS REMOVED, CUT IN STRIPS

1 CUP SNAP PEAS, TRIMMED

1 BUNCH SWISS CHARD, TRIMMED AND CHOPPED

1 POUND COLORFUL PASTA   ✳ *(Makes 6 serv-*

1. Start boiling water for the pasta.
2. In a medium saucepan or skillet, sauté the onion and garlic in olive oil for 5 minutes. Add the wine, basil, sea salt, and the remaining veggies and cook on medium heat for 10–15 minutes, until the veggies are just soft.
3. Meanwhile, cook the pasta. When it's ready, drain it, add it to the veggies, and cook for another 5 minutes. Serve hot.

Lo Mein

A colorful dish of veggies and noodles. The water chestnuts make it crunchy. The soy sauce and toasted sesame oil give it a distinctive Chinese flavor. It's difficult to find fresh Asian noodles without eggs or chemicals, but if you can find them, they make this dish particularly special.

2 QUARTS WATER

1 POUND FRESH WHEAT NOODLES

3–4 TABLESPOONS SOY SAUCE

2 TABLESPOONS RICE WINE

1 TABLESPOON TOASTED SESAME OIL

1 ONION, DICED

2 CLOVES GARLIC, MINCED

2 TABLESPOONS GRATED GINGER

3 CARROTS, SLICED

2 ZUCCHINI, SLICED

1 BABY BOK CHOY, SHREDDED

1 SMALL CAN SLICED WATER CHESTNUTS   ✳ *(Makes 6 servings)*

1. Bring the water to a boil in a medium saucepan. Turn off the heat, add the noodles and soak them for 2–3 minutes, then drain them.
2. Combine the soy sauce, rice wine, and toasted sesame oil. Pour one third of this mixture in a medium wok or skillet and sauté the onion, garlic, and ginger until the onion is soft. If it starts to stick add a few tablespoons of water.
3. Add the carrots, cook for another 3–5 minutes, then add the zucchini, bok choy, and water chestnuts and cook until the vegetables are tender. Remove them from the wok and set them aside.
4. Pour the remaining soy sauce mixture into the wok and bring it to a boil. Add the drained noodles, tossing them with tongs or chopsticks until they absorb all of the liquid. Toss the noodles with the vegetables and serve.

Southeast Asian Greens and Noodles

Mint, basil, and lime make a light and refreshing sauce for this noodle dish.

2 QUARTS WATER

1 POUND FRESH WHEAT NOODLES

1 ONION, CHOPPED

2 CLOVES GARLIC, MINCED

1 TABLESPOON GRATED GINGER

1 TABLESPOON OLIVE OIL

1 BUNCH COLLARD GREENS, CHOPPED

1 CUP CHOPPED BOK CHOY CABBAGE

1 BUNCH SPINACH, CLEANED AND TRIMMED

1 BUNCH MUSTARD GREENS, CHOPPED

1 CUP FRESH BASIL LEAVES

1/2 CUP FRESH MINT LEAVES

3–4 TABLESPOONS SOY SAUCE

2–3 TABLESPOONS WATER

2–3 TABLESPOONS LIME JUICE

✳ *(Makes 6 servings)*

1. Bring the water to a boil in a medium saucepan. Turn off the heat, add the noodles and soak them for 2–3 minutes, then drain them.
2. Meanwhile, sauté the onion, garlic, and ginger in olive oil in a medium wok or skillet. When the onion is soft add the greens, herbs, soy sauce, and water.
3. Cook until the greens are soft (collards take the longest), then add the noodles and lime juice. Toss with tongs until it's all well mixed and the noodles have soaked up the liquid.

Pad Thai

I think Pad Thai is one of the world's great dishes. The purple cabbage, orange carrots, and chopped peanuts top a mound of elegantly flavored noodles.

2 CLOVES GARLIC, MINCED

1 TABLESPOON VEGETABLE OIL

2 TABLESPOONS TOMATO PASTE

1 TABLESPOON TAMARIND CONCENTRATE

1 TABLESPOON LIME JUICE

3 TABLESPOONS SOY SAUCE

1 TEASPOON RAW SUGAR

1/4 POUND FIRM TOFU, CUT IN STRIPS

2 QUARTS WATER

1 POUND BROAD RICE NOODLES (THE ONES FROM THAILAND WORK BEST IN THIS RECIPE.)

2 CARROTS, GRATED

3 GREEN ONIONS, CHOPPED

2 CUPS SHREDDED RED CABBAGE

1 CUP BEAN SPROUTS

1/2 CUP CHOPPED ROASTED PEANUTS, SKINS OFF   ✳ *(Makes 6 servings)*

1. In a small saucepan, sauté the garlic in oil then add the tomato paste, tamarind, lime juice, soy sauce, sugar, and tofu.
2. Bring the water to a boil in a medium saucepan. Turn off the heat, add the noodles, and soak them for 2–3 minutes.
3. Drain the noodles, transfer them to a serving bowl, then pour the sauce over them and mix well.
4. Top with the raw veggies and peanuts.

Yakisoba

Noodles and veggies, Japanese style.

2 QUARTS WATER

1 POUND FRESH WHEAT NOODLES

3 TABLESPOONS SOY SAUCE

2 TABLESPOONS RICE VINEGAR

1 TEASPOON RAW SUGAR OR HONEY

1 TABLESPOON OLIVE OIL

1 ONION, CHOPPED

2 TABLESPOONS GRATED GINGER

2 CLOVES GARLIC, MINCED

2 CARROTS, GRATED

1 SMALL NAPA CABBAGE, SHREDDED   ✳ *(Makes 6 servings)*

1. Bring the water to a boil in a medium saucepan. Turn off the heat, add the noodles, and soak them for 3 minutes, then drain them.
2. Mix the soy sauce, rice vinegar, sugar, and olive oil in a bowl.
3. In a medium wok or skillet, sauté the onion, ginger, and garlic in 1–2 tablespoons of this sauce. When the onion is soft, add the carrots and cabbage, and cook until the cabbage is reduced in size.
4. Remove the veggies from the pan. Bring the remaining sauce to a boil, add the drained noodles, and toss them with tongs or chopsticks until the liquid is absorbed.
5. Mix the vegetables with the noodles and serve.

Indonesian Nuts and Noodles

The mixed nuts make this meal crunchy, unusual, and full of protein.

2 QUARTS WATER

1 POUND FRESH WHEAT NOODLES

3 TABLESPOONS SOY SAUCE

1 TABLESPOON MOLASSES

1 TABLESPOON TOASTED SESAME OIL

1 ONION, CHOPPED

1–2 TABLESPOONS GRATED GINGER

2 CLOVES GARLIC, MINCED

1/2 CUP DRY ROASTED CASHEWS

1/2 CUP DRY ROASTED PEANUTS

1/2 CUP DRY ROASTED HAZELNUTS

1 CUP BEAN SPROUTS   ✳ *(Makes 6 servings)*

1. Bring the water to a boil in a medium saucepan. Turn off the heat, add the noodles and soak them for 3 minutes, then drain them.
2. Heat the soy sauce, molasses, and toasted sesame oil in a medium wok or skillet. Add the onion, ginger, and garlic and cook for 3–5 minutes.
3. Chop the nuts coarsely in a food processor, then add them to the wok, along with the sprouts.
4. Cook for another few minutes, then add the drained noodles and toss them with tongs or chopsticks until the liquid is absorbed.

Stuffed Shells

The sauce, tofu-spinach filling, and faux cheese give this dish the look and feel of a traditional Italian casserole.

1 POUND FROZEN SPINACH

1 POUND TOFU, SOFT OR FIRM

1 TABLESPOON OLIVE OIL

1 TEASPOON SEA SALT

1 POUND PASTA SHELLS

WATER TO COVER

1 BATCH TOMATO SAUCE (PAGE **169**)

1 BATCH FAUX CHEESE (PAGE **182**)   ✳ *(Makes 6–8 servings)*

1. Preheat the oven to 350 degrees.
2. Steam the spinach until it softens.
3. Crumble the tofu and blend it in a food processor with the oil and sea salt. Transfer it to a bowl and mix in the spinach.
4. Boil the shells until they're softened but not thoroughly cooked. Drain them and rinse them in cold water.
5. Line the bottom of a casserole pan with a layer of tomato sauce.
6. Stuff the shells with the tofu-spinach mixture and arrange them on top of the sauce. Spoon the remaining sauce on top of them, and top with the faux cheese.
7. Bake 15 minutes covered and 10 minutes uncovered. Serve hot.

Greek Lasagna

The Greek seasonings in this casserole give a lively twist to a traditional lasagna. It is familiar enough and different enough to surprise and delight people.

1 ONION, CHOPPED

2–6 CLOVES GARLIC, MINCED

1 TABLESPOON OLIVE OIL

3 TABLESPOONS CHOPPED FRESH DILL OR **1** TABLESPOON DRIED

1 SMALL FENNEL BULB, CHOPPED

1 1/2 TEASPOONS SEA SALT, DIVIDED

1/2 TEASPOON BLACK PEPPER

1 CAN (**28** OZ.) CRUSHED TOMATOES

2–3 TABLESPOONS LEMON JUICE

1 POUND GREEN LASAGNA NOODLES

WATER TO COVER

1 POUND TOFU, SOFT OR FIRM

1 POUND FROZEN SPINACH, STEAMED OR THAWED

1/2 CUP CHOPPED WALNUTS

1/2 CUP PITTED CALAMATA OLIVES, CHOPPED FINELY

1 CUP FAUX CHEESE (PAGE **182**)   ✳ *(Makes 6–8 servings)*

1. In a medium saucepan, sauté the onion and garlic in the olive oil until the onion is soft. Add the dill, fennel, 1 teaspoon sea salt, and the black pepper, and cook 3–5 minutes. Mix in the canned tomatoes and simmer for 10–15 minutes, then remove the sauce from the heat and add the lemon juice.
2. Boil the lasagna noodles in water until they're tender.
3. Preheat the oven to 375 degrees.
4. Crumble the tofu or purée it in a food processor. Mix it with the spinach, walnuts, calamata olives, and the remaining 1/2 teaspoon sea salt.
5. Line the bottom of a medium casserole pan with sauce, then layer one-third of the pasta, half the spinach and tofu, half the walnuts and olives, and one-third of the remaining sauce. Then spread half the remaining pasta, the remaining spinach, tofu, walnuts and olives, and half the remaining sauce. Top this with the rest of the pasta and sauce, and the faux cheese.
6. Bake, covered, for 15 minutes, then uncover and bake another 10 minutes. Serve hot.

Pesto Lasagna

You can never have too many different kinds of lasagna. This one has a rich pesto filling.

12–15 LASAGNA NOODLES

WATER TO COVER

2 POUNDS SOFT TOFU

1 BATCH PESTO (PAGE 171)

1 BATCH TOMATO SAUCE (PAGE 169)

1 BATCH FAUX CHEESE (PAGE 182)   ✳ *(Makes 6 servings)*

1. Preheat the oven to 350 degrees.
2. Boil the lasagna noodles in water until they're tender.
3. Meanwhile, crumble the tofu with your hands or with a potato masher. Mix the pesto with the tofu.
4. When the noodles are ready, spoon one-third of the tomato sauce into a medium casserole pan and cover it with one-third of the noodles. Cover this with half the tofu mix, then half the remaining noodles and half the remaining sauce. Spread the remaining tofu, then the remaining noodles and the remaining sauce. Spoon on the faux cheese and cover the top.
5. Bake for 30 minutes.

Pasta with Olives, Artichokes, and Dried Tomatoes

Pasta with fragrant basil, crunchy almonds, and sensual artichokes.

1 POUND COLORFUL PASTA

WATER TO COVER

2 TABLESPOONS OLIVE OIL

2 CLOVES GARLIC, MINCED

3 TABLESPOONS CHOPPED FRESH BASIL

3 TABLESPOONS CHOPPED ALMONDS, WITH SKINS

1/4 CUP WHITE WINE

1/4 CUP PITTED CALAMATA OLIVES, SLICED IN THIRDS

1 CAN QUARTERED ARTICHOKE HEARTS, DRAINED

10–12 DRIED TOMATOES, COOKED FOR A MINUTE IN BOILING WATER, THEN CHOPPED

1 TEASPOON SEA SALT

1/2 TEASPOON BLACK PEPPER   ✳ *(Makes 6 servings)*

1. Cook and drain the pasta.
2. In a medium saucepan, heat the olive oil and garlic. Cook on low heat for 3–4 minutes, then add the remaining ingredients and cook another 5–10 minutes.
3. Add the pasta and mix well. Cook for another 2–3 minutes, then serve.

Dev's Basic Curry

I call this my "basic" curry because it is simple and tasty, with everything it needs and nothing more.

2 MEDIUM RED POTATOES, NOT PEELED, CHOPPED

1/2 CUP VEGGIE STOCK OR WATER

1 ONION, DICED

2 TABLESPOONS MINCED GARLIC

2 TABLESPOONS GRATED GINGER

1 TEASPOON GROUND CUMIN

1 TEASPOON GROUND CORIANDER

1 TEASPOON GROUND TURMERIC

1/2 TEASPOON ANISE OR FENNEL SEED (OPTIONAL)

1/2 TEASPOON GROUND CARDAMOM

PINCH CAYENNE (OPTIONAL)

1 TEASPOON SEA SALT

2 CARROTS, CHOPPED

1 HEAD CAULIFLOWER, BROKEN INTO BITE-SIZED PIECES

2 CUPS BROCCOLI FLORETS

1 TOMATO, DICED

1 CAN (14 OZ.) GARBANZO BEANS, DRAINED, OR 2 CUPS COOKED BEANS

1–2 TABLESPOONS LEMON JUICE

2 TABLESPOONS COCONUT MILK   ✳ *(Makes 6 servings)*

1. Steam or boil the potatoes.
2. While they're cooking, heat the stock or water in a medium saucepan, then add the onion, garlic, ginger, and seasonings, and let them cook for 5 minutes.
3. Add the carrots and cauliflower, and sauté until they're tender, with additional stock or water if necessary.
4. Add the broccoli and tomato, and cook another 3 minutes, then add the garbanzo beans, cooked potatoes, lemon juice, and coconut milk. Cook for another 2 minutes on medium heat and serve.

Spring Veggie Curry

1 ONION, CHOPPED

2 CLOVES GARLIC, MINCED

1 TABLESPOON GRATED GINGER

1 TEASPOON SEA SALT

1 TEASPOON GROUND CUMIN

1 TEASPOON GROUND TURMERIC

1 TEASPOON GROUND CORIANDER

1/2 TEASPOON GROUND CARDAMOM

1 TABLESPOON OLIVE OIL

1 TOMATO, CHOPPED OR **1/2** CUP CANNED CRUSHED TOMATO

1 BUNCH ASPARAGUS, CUT IN BITE-SIZED PIECES

1 RED BELL PEPPER, CUT IN BITE-SIZED PIECES

1/2 POUND SNAP PEAS, TRIMMED

1 BUNCH SWISS CHARD, CLEANED, TRIMMED, AND CHOPPED

1/4 CUP COCONUT MILK   ✳ *(Makes 6 serv-*

1. In a medium skillet or saucepan, sauté the onion, garlic, ginger, sea salt, and spices in olive oil for five minutes or until the onion is soft.
2. Add the tomato and the remaining veggies and cook on medium-low heat for another 10 minutes, then add the coconut milk, heat through, and serve.

Pea and Potato Curry

This dish is simple and satisfying, and also makes a great filling for samosas (East Indian turnovers). Serve with Tamarind-Date Chutney (page 181). Don't use russet potatoes for this dish, they crumble. You want potatoes that will hold their shape.

4 MEDIUM RED OR YELLOW POTATOES, NOT PEELED, CHOPPED

1 ONION, CHOPPED

2 CLOVES GARLIC, MINCED

1 TABLESPOON GRATED GINGER

1 TOMATO, CHOPPED

1 TEASPOON SEA SALT

1 TEASPOON GROUND CUMIN

1/2 TEASPOON GROUND CORIANDER

1/2 TEASPOON GROUND TURMERIC

1/2 TEASPOON GROUND CARDAMOM

1 TABLESPOON OLIVE OIL

2/3 CUP FROZEN PEAS

1–2 TABLESPOONS LEMON JUICE   ✳ *(Makes 4–6 servings)*

1. Boil the potatoes for 10 minutes, until they're soft.
2. In a medium saucepan or skillet, sauté the onion, garlic, ginger, tomato, sea salt, and spices in olive oil until the onion is soft.
3. Add the remaining ingredients and heat through.

Winter Veggie Curry

This curry uses a rich variety of winter veggies. It is filling and satisfying.

1 TABLESPOON GRATED GINGER

2 CLOVES GARLIC, MINCED

2 LEEKS, SLICED LENGTHWISE, CLEANED, AND CHOPPED

1 TABLESPOON OLIVE OIL

1 TEASPOON SEA SALT

1 TEASPOON GROUND CUMIN

1 TEASPOON GROUND TURMERIC

1 TEASPOON GROUND CORIANDER

1/2 TEASPOON GROUND CARDAMOM

2 PARSNIPS, CHOPPED

2 CARROTS, CHOPPED

1 BUNCH KALE, CLEANED AND CHOPPED

1 YAM, PEELED AND CUT IN BITE-SIZED CHUNKS

1/2 CUP VEGGIE STOCK OR WATER

CAYENNE TO TASTE   ✳ *(Makes 6 serv-*

1. In a medium skillet or saucepan, sauté the ginger, garlic, and leeks in olive oil with the sea salt and spices.
2. Add the remaining veggies, along with the stock or water, and cook, covered, until the yam and parsnip are soft, about 10–15 minutes. Add the cayenne, stir, and serve.

Palak Tofu

I've substituted tofu for cheese cubes in this traditional Indian dish. You can substitute one tablespoon of curry for the four ground spices.

1 PACKAGE (**10** OZ.) FROZEN SPINACH, OR **1** BUNCH FRESH, CLEANED AND CHOPPED, STEMS REMOVED

1 ONION, CHOPPED

2 CLOVES GARLIC, MINCED

1 TABLESPOON GRATED GINGER

1 TEASPOON GROUND CUMIN

1/2 TEASPOON GROUND TURMERIC

1/2 TEASPOON GROUND CORIANDER

1/2 TEASPOON GROUND CARDAMOM

1 TEASPOON SEA SALT

CAYENNE TO TASTE

1 TABLESPOON OLIVE OIL

1/2 POUND FIRM OR EXTRA FIRM TOFU, CUBED

1 TOMATO, CHOPPED   ✳ *(Makes 6 serv-*

1. Steam the spinach until it's wilted or thawed.
2. In a medium skillet or saucepan, sauté the onion, garlic, ginger, spices, and sea salt in olive oil until the onion is soft, about 5 minutes.
3. Add the spinach, tofu, and tomato, mix gently, and cook another 5 minutes, stirring often.

Tamales

The food we now know as a tamale was once a religious offering, a gift the Aztecs brought to their gods, tied in corn husk wrappers. Over time they grew into preparation for a family feast on Christmas or New Year's. The elder mixes the masa — a technique she has been perfecting for many years — and relatives and friends assemble the tamales. Because they are formed by hand, every tamale is individual. You can pick out each person's style as you steam the assembled tomatoes.

A tamale can be wrapped in a corn husk, or a banana or avocado leaf. Wrappers vary from region to region. The dough is made from ground corn with a trace of limestone, and either mixed fresh or prepared from masa harina, an instant corn meal mixture. Lard is the traditional shortening; it makes the tamales especially light and fluffy, but you can get good results with corn oil or olive oil.

This year my company sold tamales at farmers' markets. They are a wonderful street food: steamy and comforting on cool days, satisfying but never too filling on hot days. People come up to our booth every week and tell stories about the gatherings of friends and neighbors and the places they recalled when they smelled the tamales steaming.

Every Thursday we came together as a group to make them for the weekend. The oldest and wisest member of our company naturally gravitated toward the task of mixing the masa. He does the best job and takes the most pride in the task, setting the pace, maintaining the heartbeat. None of us knew, until very recently, that this was the traditional role of the elder in the tamale-making process.

Assembling Tamales

1 TEASPOON SEA SALT

1 TABLESPOON CANOLA, CORN, OR OLIVE OIL

2 CUPS WATER

2 CUPS MASA HARINA OR MASA MIXTA

15 CORN HUSKS   ✳ *(Makes 15 tamales)*

1. Prepare the filling of your choice—see pages 92 and 93. In a saucepan, add the sea salt and oil to the water and bring it to a boil.
2. Add one cup of masa mix and whisk until it's somewhat smooth. Add the second cup of masa. When it gets too thick for the whisk, continue stirring with a spatula.
3. Spread the mixture 1–2 inches thick on a baking pan. Leave it until it is just cool enough to handle, about 5–10 minutes.
4. Soak the husks in hot water.
5. When the masa mixture is cool enough to handle, roll it into golf balls. Wet your hands when they get sticky.
6. Open a corn husk so it looks like a fan. Place a ball of masa in the center, flatten the ball, and lay a spoonful of filling in the middle. Fold the sides of the husk so they meet. This should close the flattened masa around the filling. Press it together.
7. Unfold the husk, then fold the bottom up and the sides together to close the tamale. If the husk isn't big enough to cover the masa, tie a piece of string around it to hold it closed. Repeat with the remaining husks and masa.
8. Steam the tamales for 15 minutes.

Tamale Fillings

Mix all the ingredients in these fillings.

Chile, Tomato, and Corn Filling

1 MEDIUM TOMATO, CHOPPED IN **1/2**-INCH PIECES

1 SMALL CAN DICED GREEN CHILES

1 CUP FROZEN CORN KERNELS

2 TABLESPOONS RED WINE VINEGAR

1 TEASPOON SEA SALT   ✳ *(Makes 15 tamales)*

Chipotle Filling

3 CANNED CHIPOTLE (SMOKED JALAPEÑOS), FINELY CHOPPED, WITH THEIR SAUCE

8 DRIED TOMATOES, SOAKED IN HOT WATER AND FINELY CHOPPED

2 CUPS COOKED KIDNEY, PINTO, OR BLACK BEANS

1 TEASPOON SEA SALT

2 TABLESPOONS RED WINE VINEGAR   ✳ *(Makes 15 tamales)*

Squash and Olive Filling

1 ACORN SQUASH, HALVED, SEEDS REMOVED, AND BAKED, FLESH MASHED

1/2 CUP CHOPPED ALMONDS, WITH SKINS

1/2 CUP CHOPPED BLACK OLIVES

1 TEASPOON SEA SALT

2 TABLESPOONS RED WINE VINEGAR

1 TEASPOON CHILI POWDER

1/2 TEASPOON GROUND CUMIN

1/2 TEASPOON DRIED OREGANO   ✳ *(Makes 15 tamales)*

Spinach and Pumpkin Seed Filling

1 PACKAGE **(10** OZ.**)** FROZEN SPINACH, DEFROSTED

1/2 CUP SKINNED, ROASTED PUMPKIN SEEDS

3 TABLESPOONS CHOPPED CILANTRO

1–2 TABLESPOONS LIME JUICE

1 TEASPOON SEA SALT   ✳ *(Makes 15 tamales)*

Tamale Pie

Here is the stone ground corn flavor of tamales without the work of individually assembling them.

3 CUPS WATER, DIVIDED

1 TABLESPOON OLIVE OIL

1 TEASPOON SEA SALT

2 CUPS MASA HARINA OR MASA MIXTA

10–12 DRIED TOMATOES

3 CANNED CHIPOTLE (SMOKED JALAPEÑOS) AND THEIR SAUCE

2 CUPS COOKED BLACK OR PINTO BEANS

1 TABLESPOON RED WINE VINEGAR

1 TEASPOON SEA SALT

1/2 BATCH RED CHILE SALSA (PAGE **180**)

1/2 BATCH FAUX CHEESE (PAGE **182**)   ✳ *(Makes 6–8 servings)*

1. Preheat the oven to 375 degrees.
2. In a small saucepan, bring 2 cups of water to a boil and add the olive oil and sea salt. Turn off the heat and add the masa immediately. Stir until it's smooth. Spoon half of it into a casserole pan and spread it over the bottom and up the sides.
3. Cook the dried tomatoes in the remaining water for a minute or two, then drain them and chop them finely.
4. Chop the chipotle and mix them with the beans, chopped dried tomatoes, vinegar, and sea salt. Use this mixture to fill the masa shell you just made.
5. Flatten handfuls of the remaining half of the masa and use them to cover the beans. (You can't roll it.) Don't worry about making the pieces of masa match perfectly.
6. Top the masa with the salsa, then faux cheese.
7. Bake for 20–30 minutes, until the top starts to brown. Serve.

Enchilada Pie

This dish is easier than enchiladas since no rolling is involved.

2 CUPS PINTO BEANS

WATER TO COVER

1 ONION, CHOPPED

2 CLOVES GARLIC, MINCED

1 ANAHEIM CHILE, DICED, OR 2 TABLESPOONS CANNED DICED GREEN CHILES

1 TABLESPOON CHILI POWDER

1 TEASPOON DRIED OREGANO

1 TEASPOON GROUND CUMIN

1 TEASPOON SEA SALT

TABASCO TO TASTE

1 ZUCCHINI, CHOPPED

1 GREEN BELL PEPPER, CHOPPED (OPTIONAL)

1/2 CUP FROZEN CORN

1 BATCH RED CHILE SALSA (PAGE 180)

1/2 BATCH FAUX CHEESE (PAGE 182)

1 PACKAGE CORN TORTILLAS   ✳ *(Makes 6–8 servings)*

1. Preheat the oven to 375 degrees.
2. Soak the beans overnight in water, then boil them in a medium saucepan for at least an hour with the onion, garlic, chiles, seasonings, sea salt, and Tabasco.
3. Add the zucchini and green bell pepper, if using, and continue cooking on medium heat until the beans are so tender they break when you stir them. Add the corn and mix the beans well, mashing them.
4. Spread a layer of salsa on the bottom of a casserole pan, then spread tortillas to cover it. Spoon half the bean mixture on top, then spread another layer each of tortillas, salsa, and beans. Cover the top with the remaining tortillas, then salsa and faux cheese.
5. Bake for 20–30 minutes, until the faux cheese starts to brown.

Spanakopita

Crispy layers of filo dough stuffed with a tangy, hearty lentil filling.

1 PACKAGE FILO DOUGH

1 PACKAGE FROZEN SPINACH OR **1** BUNCH SPINACH, CLEANED AND TRIMMED

1 ONION, CHOPPED

3–6 CLOVES GARLIC, MINCED

1/2 CUP OLIVE OIL, DIVIDED

2 CUPS COOKED LENTILS

1–2 TABLESPOONS LEMON JUICE

1 POUND TOFU, SOFT OR FIRM, CRUMBLED

2 TEASPOONS SEA SALT

1 TEASPOON DRIED DILL

1/2 TEASPOON ANISE SEED (OPTIONAL)   ✳ *(Makes 12 servings)*

1. Defrost the filo dough a day before you need it, then leave the package at room temperature while you prepare the other ingredients.
2. Preheat the oven to 375 degrees.
3. Steam the spinach until it's wilted or thawed.
4. In a medium skillet, sauté the onion and garlic in 1 tablespoon olive oil, then add the spinach, lentils, lemon juice, tofu, and seasonings.
5. Use a pastry brush to brush a layer of olive oil on the bottom of a baking pan. Lay a sheet of filo dough over it, brush it with oil, and repeat with 10–12 sheets. Don't agonize if some sheets stick together. The final product will look fine.
6. Spread the filling over the first 10–12 sheets, then layer and brush the remaining filo dough on top of the filling. Score it into twelve pieces by cutting just to the filling. Make three pieces across and four down.
7. Bake, covered with aluminum foil, for 15 minutes, then uncover and cook another 10 minutes.
8. Serve warm or cold.

Sesame Baked Tofu

I eat this tofu with rice and steamed greens. It makes a very grounding meal.

1/3 CUP TAHINI

1/2 CUP SOY SAUCE

1/3 CUP NUTRITIONAL YEAST

2 TABLESPOONS RICE VINEGAR

1 POUND FIRM TOFU   ✳ *(Makes 3–4 servings)*

1. Preheat the oven to 375 degrees.
2. Mix all the ingredients except the tofu in a bowl.
3. Slice the tofu in slices 1/4 inch thick. Dip each slice in the sauce, then spread the tofu on an oiled baking sheet.
4. Bake for 30 minutes.

Spinach and Tofu in Peanut Sauce

This is a lovely, layered dish with crunchy tofu and spicy peanut sauce on a bed of fresh spinach. Serve with rice or rice noodles.

OIL FOR DEEP FRYING

1/2 POUND FIRM TOFU

1/4 CUP WHOLE WHEAT PASTRY FLOUR (OR WHATEVER FLOUR YOU HAVE ON HAND)

1 BUNCH SPINACH, CLEANED AND TRIMMED

1 BATCH PEANUT SAUCE (PAGE 176)   ✻ (Makes 3–4 servings)

1. In a small skillet, heat the oil on medium-low heat.
2. Cut the tofu in bite-sized cubes and roll the pieces in flour. When the oil is hot enough that you can bounce a drop of oil off its surface, fry the tofu for about 5 minutes, until it's golden brown.
3. Meanwhile, steam the spinach until it's just wilted.
4. Arrange the spinach on a plate, put the tofu on top, and pour the peanut sauce on top.

Skewered Veggies in Thai BBQ Sauce

There's something primeval about the experience of eating food roasted on a stick, not to mention the fact that roasting and grilling draw out the finest flavor in a vegetable. You'll need 10–12 wooden skewers.

SAUCE:

1 CUP TOMATO JUICE

1 TABLESPOON COCONUT MILK (OPTIONAL)

1 TEASPOON GRATED GINGER

1 TABLESPOON LIME JUICE

1 TABLESPOON CHOPPED FRESH BASIL

2 TABLESPOONS SOY SAUCE

VEGGIES:

1 ZUCCHINI, CHOPPED

8–12 SMALL MUSHROOMS

1 GREEN BELL PEPPER, CUT IN STRIPS

1 RED BELL PEPPER, CUT IN STRIPS

1 CUP BROCCOLI FLORETS

1 CUP CAULIFLOWER FLORETS

1 RED ONION, QUARTERED AND SEPARATED
INTO LAYERS

✳ *(Makes 10–12 skewers)*

1. Preheat the oven to 400 degrees, or if you're going to grill on an open flame, soak the skewers in warm water while you prepare the food.
2. Mix the sauce.
3. Marinate the veggies in the sauce, ideally for at least a half hour.
4. Poke holes in the veggies and arrange a variety on each skewer. Pay attention to the colors.
5. Roast them on a baking pan for 20 minutes, or grill them outdoors on a barbecue until they start to brown.

Chinese Veggies
with Black Bean Sauce

Chinese food is characterized by subtle interplay of color, flavor, and texture. This mixed vegetable dish has a sweet, sour, salty sauce and a plentiful array of vegetables.

1 ONION, CHOPPED

1 TABLESPOON GRATED GINGER

2 CLOVES GARLIC, CHOPPED

1/2 CUP VEGGIE STOCK, OR **2** TABLESPOONS OLIVE OIL

2 CARROTS, CHOPPED

2 ZUCCHINI, CHOPPED

1 CUP CHOPPED GREEN BEANS

1 SMALL BOK CHOY, SHREDDED

8–12 MUSHROOMS, CHOPPED

1 GREEN BELL PEPPER, CHOPPED

1 CUP BEAN SPROUTS

1 SMALL CAN SLICED WATER CHESTNUTS, DRAINED

1 SMALL CAN SLICED BAMBOO SHOOTS, DRAINED

1 BATCH BLACK BEAN SAUCE (PAGE **174**)   ✳ *(Makes 4–6 servings)*

1. In a medium wok or skillet, sauté the onion, ginger, and garlic in the stock or oil until the onion is soft.
2. Add the carrots and cook another 3–5 minutes, then add the remaining fresh veggies and cook another 8–10 minutes.
3. Add the remaining ingredients and cook another 5 minutes or so.

Indonesian Stir-Fry

Soy sauce, molasses, and toasted sesame oil make a sweet, musky sauce for these nuts and veggies.

8 OUNCES TEMPEH, CUBED

1 TABLESPOON OLIVE OIL

1 TABLESPOON GRATED GINGER

2 CLOVES GARLIC, MINCED

1 ONION, DICED

1/2 CUP STOCK, DIVIDED

2 CARROTS, CHOPPED

2 TABLESPOONS SOY SAUCE

1 BABY BOK CHOY, CHOPPED

1 CUP BEAN SPROUTS

1/4 CUP CHOPPED HAZELNUTS

1 TABLESPOON MOLASSES

1 TEASPOON TOASTED SESAME OIL ✳ *(Makes 4–6 servings)*

1. In a medium wok or skillet, brown the tempeh in the olive oil.
2. Add the ginger, garlic, onion, and half the stock. Sauté until the onion is soft, then add the carrots and soy sauce.
3. After 5 minutes add the bok choy and remaining stock.
4. When the bok choy cooks down a bit add the remaining ingredients and cook a few more minutes.

Mushroom Polenta Casserole

A polenta torte with a layer of herbs and mixed mushrooms in the middle.

1 POUND BUTTON MUSHROOMS, QUARTERED

1/2 POUND MIXTURE OF SHITAKE, PORTABELLO, OYSTER, AND/OR CHANTERELLE MUSHROOMS, SLICED

2 CLOVES GARLIC, MINCED

3 SHALLOTS, CHOPPED

1/2 CUP WHITE WINE

2 TABLESPOONS OLIVE OIL, DIVIDED

1–2 TEASPOONS SEA SALT, DIVIDED

1 BUNCH SWISS CHARD, CLEANED AND CHOPPED, STEMS REMOVED

4 1/2 CUPS WATER

1 1/2 CUPS POLENTA

1/2 TEASPOON DRIED THYME

1/2 TEASPOON DRIED TARRAGON

1/2 TEASPOON DRIED MARJORAM   ✳ *(Makes 6 servings)*

1. Preheat the oven to 350 degrees.
2. In a medium saucepan, sauté the mushrooms, garlic, and shallots in wine and 1 tablespoon olive oil, along with half the sea salt. When the shallots are soft, add the chard, cover the pan, and lower the heat.
3. Boil the water with the remaining sea salt and olive oil, then reduce the heat and stir in the polenta, stirring almost constantly.
4. When the polenta thickens, add the herbs and pour half the polenta mixture into a casserole pan. Let it sit for 5 minutes, then pour on the mushroom, garlic, and shallot mixture.
5. Stir the remaining polenta, then spoon or pour it on top.
6. Bake for 15–20 minutes, until the casserole is heated through.

Sweet Potato Pot Pie

I adore this recipe. Polenta on the bottom, curried lentils in the middle, and yams on top. It's great for Thanksgiving, or any day.

FILLING:

2 CUPS LENTILS

6 CUPS WATER

1 TABLESPOON GRATED GINGER

3 CLOVES GARLIC, MINCED

1 CUP CANNED CRUSHED TOMATOES OR TOMATO PURÉE

1 ONION, CHOPPED

1 TEASPOON GROUND CINNAMON

1 TEASPOON GROUND CUMIN

1 TEASPOON GROUND CORIANDER

1 TEASPOON SEA SALT

BOTTOM LAYER:

3 CUPS WATER

1 CUP POLENTA

1 TABLESPOON OLIVE OIL

1 TEASPOON SEA SALT

TOP LAYER:

6 YAMS, BAKED UNTIL SOFT

1/2 TEASPOON SEA SALT

✳ *(Makes 6 servings)*

1. To make the filling, boil the lentils in the water in a medium saucepan. Add the other filling ingredients and cook for about 45 minutes, until the lentils are soft.
2. Preheat the oven to 350 degrees.
3. To make the bottom layer, in a small saucepan, boil the water for the polenta and add the olive oil and sea salt. When the water boils, reduce the heat and drizzle in the polenta, stirring constantly until it thickens. Pour it into the bottom of a casserole pan and let it set.
4. To make the top layer, peel and mash the yams, adding the sea salt.
5. When the lentils are ready, pour them over the polenta. Smooth the yams on top.
6. Bake for fifteen minutes or until the pot pie is heated through, and serve.

Collard Greens and Black-Eyed Peas

Here is my version of the Southern comfort food.

2 CUPS BLACK-EYED PEAS

4 CUPS WATER

3 CLOVES GARLIC, MINCED

SEA SALT TO TASTE

3 TABLESPOONS VEGAN WORCESTERSHIRE (PAGE **178**)

1 BUNCH COLLARD GREENS, CLEANED AND CHOPPED

TABASCO TO TASTE   ✳ *(Makes 4 servings)*

1. In a medium saucepan, cook the black-eyed peas in the water along with the garlic, sea salt, and Worcestershire for about 30 minutes.
2. Add the collard greens and cook for another 20–30 minutes.
3. Add the Tabasco and serve.

Cajun Red Beans and Rice

This is a vegetarian version of the Cajun staple. Soysage and liquid smoke call to mind the Southern flavors.

---

1 ONION, CHOPPED

2 CLOVES GARLIC, MINCED

1 GREEN BELL PEPPER, CHOPPED

1 TABLESPOON OLIVE OIL

1 1/2 CUPS COOKED SMALL RED BEANS

1 1/2 CUPS COOKED BROWN RICE

2 TABLESPOONS VEGAN WORCESTERSHIRE (PAGE **178**)

1 TEASPOON SEA SALT

1/4 POUND SOYSAGE, CHOPPED

1/2 TEASPOON LIQUID SMOKE

TABASCO TO TASTE   ✳ *(Makes 4 servings)*

---

1. In a medium skillet or saucepan, sauté the onion, garlic, and green bell pepper in olive oil. Cook for 5–10 minutes until the onion is soft.
2. Add the remaining ingredients and heat through.

Spanish Veggie Stew

Here is a tomato-based stew, full of veggies, with the added ripe flavor of green olives.

1 ONION, CHOPPED

2 CLOVES GARLIC, MINCED

1 TABLESPOON OLIVE OIL

1 TEASPOON SEA SALT

2 CARROTS, CHOPPED

1 ZUCCHINI, CHOPPED

1 BUNCH KALE, CLEANED, TRIMMED, AND CHOPPED

1 CUP FROZEN PEAS

1 CAN (28 OZ., MORE OR LESS) CRUSHED TOMATOES

1/4 CUP PITTED GREEN OLIVES, SLICED

2 TABLESPOONS CHOPPED PARSLEY ✳ *(Makes 6 servings)*

1. In a medium saucepan, sauté the onion and garlic in olive oil for 5 minutes. Add the sea salt.
2. Add the carrots and zucchini and cook another 5–10 minutes, until the carrot is soft.
3. Add the remaining ingredients and cook another 10–15 minutes, until the kale is tender.

Ground Nut Stew

This is an East African stew, where the combination of tomato and peanut butter creates a flavor quite unlike either one.

1 ONION, CHOPPED

2 CLOVES GARLIC, MINCED

1 TABLESPOON GRATED GINGER

1 EGGPLANT, CHOPPED

1 TABLESPOON OLIVE OIL

1 CUP WATER OR VEGGIE STOCK

1/2 CUP PEANUT BUTTER, CRUNCHY OR SMOOTH

2 TABLESPOONS TOMATO PASTE

1 CUP CHOPPED OKRA, FRESH OR FROZEN

1 TEASPOON SEA SALT

CAYENNE TO TASTE   ✳ *(Makes 6 servings)*

1. In a medium saucepan, sauté the onion, garlic, ginger, and eggplant in olive oil. Add a little stock or water if the eggplant sticks.
2. When the eggplant is soft, add the remaining ingredients and cook another 10–15 minutes.

Red Beans and Greens in Coconut Milk

One of my personal favorites.

1 CUP SMALL RED BEANS

WATER TO COVER

1 TEASPOON SEA SALT

1 ONION, CHOPPED

1 TOMATO, CHOPPED

1 TEASPOON GROUND TURMERIC

1 BUNCH CHOPPED KALE, COLLARDS, MUSTARD GREENS, OR A COMBINATION

2 TABLESPOONS COCONUT MILK

CAYENNE TO TASTE   ✳ *(Makes 4 serv-*

1. Cover the beans with water and soak them for a few hours or overnight. (If you don't plan ahead, just allow 20–30 minutes extra cooking time.)
2. If you've soaked the beans, change the water. Add sea salt, and cook them over medium heat in a medium saucepan.
3. After half an hour add the onion, tomato, and turmeric.
4. After another half hour add the greens and cook for another 15–20 minutes, until the beans are soft.
5. Add the coconut milk and cayenne and serve.

Squash Ratatouille

A celebration of the flavors of late summer. Serve it over polenta.

1 ACORN SQUASH

1 ONION, DICED

2 CLOVES GARLIC, MINCED

1 EGGPLANT, CUBED

1 SMALL FENNEL BULB, FINELY CHOPPED (OPTIONAL, BUT RECOMMENDED)

1 TABLESPOON DRIED OR CHOPPED FRESH BASIL

1 TEASPOON DRIED MARJORAM

1 TEASPOON DRIED TARRAGON

1/2 TEASPOON BLACK PEPPER

1 TABLESPOON OLIVE OIL

1 CAN (**28** OZ.) CRUSHED TOMATOES

1 TEASPOON SEA SALT   ✳ *(Makes 6 serv-*

1. Cut the squash in half, scoop out the seeds, and steam it for 30 minutes.
2. Meanwhile, in a medium skillet or saucepan, sauté the onion, garlic, eggplant, fennel, and seasonings in olive oil.
3. When the eggplant is soft, about 15 minutes, add the tomatoes and sea salt and cook another 20–30 minutes.
4. When the squash is soft, peel it, cut it in bite-sized pieces, and mix it with the remaining ingredients.

Acorn Squash Stuffed with Wild Rice

The taste of squash and wild rice is the flavor of autumn harvest. This makes a downright traditional Thanksgiving dish.

1 CUP WILD RICE

6 CUPS WATER

1 1/2 CUPS BROWN RICE

3 ACORN SQUASH

WATER FOR BAKING

1 ONION, CHOPPED

1 TABLESPOON OLIVE OIL

1 TEASPOON SEA SALT

1/2 TEASPOON BLACK PEPPER

1 BUNCH PARSLEY, CHOPPED

1/2 CUP BREAD CRUMBS

✳ *(Makes 6 serv-*

1. Preheat the oven to 350 degrees.
2. In a medium saucepan, cook the wild rice in the water, and add the brown rice after half an hour.
3. In the meantime, cut the squash in half, take out the seeds, and cook it on a baking sheet filled with 1/2 inch of water for 45 minutes to an hour, until it's soft. Let it sit at room temperature until it is cool enough to handle.
4. Sauté the onion in the olive oil with the sea salt and black pepper.
5. When the rice is cooked, mix it with the cooked onion, parsley, sea salt, and black pepper.
6. Scoop about half of the inside out of the squash, mash it, and mix it with the rice mixture.
7. Use this to stuff each of the squash, then top the stuffing with bread crumbs and bake for another 15 minutes.

Afghan Stew

The first time I tasted Afghan food I knew I absolutely had to learn to make it.

1 ONION, CHOPPED

2 CLOVES GARLIC, MINCED

1 MEDIUM EGGPLANT, CHOPPED

1 TABLESPOON OLIVE OIL

1 TEASPOON SEA SALT

1 TEASPOON DRIED DILL

1 TEASPOON GROUND CUMIN

1 TEASPOON DRIED MINT

1/2 TEASPOON GROUND CARDAMOM

1 TABLESPOON CHOPPED CILANTRO

2 CARROTS, CHOPPED

1 ZUCCHINI, CHOPPED

1 CUP CANNED CRUSHED TOMATOES

1 BUNCH SPINACH, CLEANED, OR **1** PACKAGE (**10** OZ.) FROZEN SPINACH, THAWED

1–2 TABLESPOONS LEMON JUICE

✳ *(Makes 6 servings)*

1. In a medium skillet or saucepan, sauté the onion, garlic, and egg-plant in olive oil with the sea salt and seasonings. Add a few table-spoons of water if the eggplant sticks to the pan.
2. When the eggplant is soft, add the carrots and, a few minutes later, the zucchini.
3. When the zucchini is soft, add the tomatoes and spinach and cook another 5 minutes.
4. Add the lemon juice and serve.

Bean and Basil Burgers

Even children enjoy these burgers. Chop all the ingredients together in a food processor or blender (if you want them to look more homogeneous). Serve them on buns, with condiments.

2 CUPS COOKED BLACK BEANS

2 CUPS COOKED BROWN RICE

3 TABLESPOONS CHOPPED BLACK OLIVES

2 TABLESPOONS CHOPPED FRESH BASIL

2 TABLESPOONS TOMATO PASTE

1/2 TEASPOON SEA SALT

1 TABLESPOON CRUSHED RED PEPPER FLAKES
(OPTIONAL)   ✳ *(Makes 8–10 generous servings)*

1. Preheat the oven to 350 degrees.
2. Mix all the ingredients.
3. Form the mixture into burgers with your hands. Wet your hands if the mixture sticks to them.
4. Bake on a greased cookie sheet for 10–15 minutes.

Kedgeree
(Lentils and Rice)

I've adapted this Middle Eastern staple by adding a variety of veggies for color and texture.

1 CUP BROWN RICE

6 CUPS WATER, DIVIDED

1 CUP LENTILS

3 CLOVES GARLIC, MINCED

1 ONION, CHOPPED

2 TABLESPOONS OLIVE OIL

3 CARROTS, CHOPPED

6–8 MUSHROOMS, QUARTERED

1 BUNCH KALE, CLEANED, TRIMMED, AND CHOPPED

1 TEASPOON GROUND CUMIN

1 TEASPOON DRY MUSTARD

1 TEASPOON SEA SALT

1–2 TABLESPOONS LEMON JUICE   ✳ *(Makes 6 servings)*

1. In a small saucepan, cook the rice in 2 cups of water.
2. In a medium saucepan, cook the lentils in the remaining 4 cups of water until they are soft, about 40–60 minutes. Drain.
3. In a medium skillet, sauté the garlic and onion in olive oil, then add the carrots, mushrooms, kale, and seasonings. Add the lentils, rice, and lemon juice.
4. Stir until it's well mixed and heated through. Serve hot.

Eggplant Parmesan

This is a vegan version of the succulent Italian favorite.

2 MEDIUM EGGPLANTS

1 POUND TOFU, SOFT OR FIRM

1 TABLESPOON OLIVE OIL

1/2 TEASPOON SEA SALT

1 POUND FROZEN SPINACH, STEAMED OR THAWED

1 BATCH TOMATO SAUCE (PAGE **169**)

1/2 BATCH FAUX CHEESE (PAGE **182**)   ✳ *(Makes 6 servings)*

1. Preheat the oven to 350 degrees.
2. Cut the eggplant in slices 1/4 inch thick. Steam them for 5–10 minutes.
3. Purée the tofu with the olive oil and sea salt, then mix in the spinach.
4. Line the bottom of a casserole pan with tomato sauce, then layer half the eggplant.
5. Spread the tofu and spinach mixture, then the remaining eggplant and sauce, then the faux cheese.
6. Bake 15 minutes covered, and 10 minutes uncovered.

4

The Many
Uses of
Seitan

Basic Seitan

Seitan is, well, a meat substitute. It is made from wheat gluten and is quite high in protein and low in fat. With the right materials it is relatively easy to make. I prefer it over tofu in many recipes because it is less likely to fall apart and it accepts flavor as well. It has been my experience, over years of feeding vegetarians, that people generally either love it or hate it. If you hate it, skip it. If you love it, you'll find a recipe that's easier than any I've read. If it's new to you, give it a try. It's quite versatile. You can store extras in the refrigerator in the broth you used to cook it. It will keep for about a week and a half.

1 GALLON WATER

CHUNK OF GINGER

1/2 CUP SOY SAUCE

1 CUP GLUTEN FLOUR (ALSO KNOWN AS HIGH GLUTEN FLOUR, OR **80%** GLUTEN FLOUR)

1–2 CUPS WARM WATER   ✳ *(Makes 2 1/2 pounds)*

1. In a large pot begin boiling the water, along with the ginger and soy sauce.
2. Mix the gluten with 1–2 cups warm water, mixing it with your hands until it becomes a sticky blob.
3. Run cold water over it and knead it underwater for a few minutes, changing the water when it gets cloudy. If the gluten you use is fresh, the dough will hold together. If the gluten is less fresh, it will break apart as you knead it. If this happens, pour the water through a wire strainer, then collect the pieces you strained out and press them back into the original blob.
4. When the water boils, cut pieces of gluten about the size of a finger and drop them into the pot. Cook for 1 1/2–2 hours.

Seitan Sate

The primeval joy of meat on a stick, vegan style.

1 POUND SEITAN, CUT IN BITE-SIZED CHUNKS

1 BATCH PEANUT SAUCE (PAGE 176)   ✳ *(Makes 12–15 skewers)*

1. Preheat the oven to 400 degrees.
2. Toss the seitan in half the peanut sauce, then poke it onto skewers, 7–8 pieces per skewer.
3. Spread them on a cookie sheet or baking pan and roast them 15–20 minutes, until they start to brown.
4. Serve with the rest of the peanut sauce.

Korean Barbecued Seitan

Marinated, roasted onions with chewy chunks of barbecued seitan.

1/2 CUP SOY SAUCE

1 TEASPOON GRATED GINGER

1 TABLESPOON BLACKSTRAP MOLASSES

1/2 TEASPOON TOASTED SESAME OIL

2 ONIONS, SLICED IN RINGS

1 RECIPE SEITAN (PAGE **127**), CUT IN BITE-SIZED CHUNKS

2 TABLESPOONS SESAME SEEDS   ❊ *(Makes 6–8 servings)*

1. Preheat the oven to 400 degrees.
2. Combine the first four ingredients.
3. Toss the onions and seitan in the mixture you've just made.
4. Spread them on a baking pan and sprinkle them with sesame seeds.
5. Roast them for 30–40 minutes, until the onions are tender and start to brown.

Seitan Cacciatore

Here the seitan stars in a tomato-based stew.

2 GREEN BELL PEPPERS, CUT IN STRIPS

2 RED BELL PEPPERS, CUT IN STRIPS

1 BATCH TOMATO SAUCE (PAGE **169**)

1 RECIPE SEITAN (PAGE **127**), CUT IN BITE-SIZED CHUNKS

1 CUP FROZEN PEAS   ✳ *(Makes 6 servings)*

1. Steam the bell peppers until they're tender.
2. Transfer them to a medium saucepan, and heat them along with the tomato sauce, seitan, and peas.

Kung Pao Seitan

Seitan, veggies, and cashews, with Chinese seasonings. Serve it with Fried Rice (page 160).

1 ONION, MINCED

2 CLOVES GARLIC, MINCED

1 TABLESPOON GRATED GINGER

1 TABLESPOON OLIVE OIL

3 TABLESPOONS SOY SAUCE

2 CARROTS, CHOPPED

1 ZUCCHINI, CHOPPED

1 CUP CHOPPED BOK CHOY

6 MUSHROOMS, QUARTERED

1 CUP CHOPPED SEITAN (PAGE **127**)

1 SMALL CAN SLICED WATER CHESTNUTS, DRAINED

1 SMALL CAN BAMBOO SHOOTS, DRAINED

1 CUP BEAN SPROUTS

1 TEASPOON TOASTED SESAME OIL

1/4 CUP CASHEWS

CHILE OIL TO TASTE   ✳ *(Makes 6 servings)*

1. In a medium skillet or saucepan, sauté the onion, garlic, and ginger in olive oil until the onion is soft.
2. Add the soy sauce and carrots, cook a few more minutes, then add the zucchini, bok choy, and mushrooms. Cook 8–10 minutes on medium heat, stirring often.
3. Add the remaining ingredients and cook another 5–10 minutes.

Thai Curry with Seitan

A Thai stir-fry, with mixed veggies and the flowery taste of lemongrass. You can substitute firm tofu for seitan in this recipe, if you prefer. If you can't find lemongrass or lime leaves, the recipe will still work.

1/2 POUND SEITAN, CUT IN BITE-SIZED PIECES

3–4 TABLESPOONS SOY SAUCE

2–3 TABLESPOONS LIME JUICE

3 STALKS LEMONGRASS, CUT IN 2- TO 3-INCH PIECES

6–8 LIME (KAFIR) LEAVES

3 TABLESPOONS GRATED GINGER

3–6 CLOVES GARLIC, MINCED

2/3 CUP VEGGIE STOCK OR WATER, DIVIDED

1 ONION, DICED

2 CARROTS, SLICED

2 CUPS CAULIFLOWER, CHOPPED

2 CUPS BROCCOLI, CHOPPED

2 ZUCCHINI, SLICED

1 BABY BOK CHOY, CHOPPED

8 MUSHROOMS, QUARTERED

1 CUP GREEN BEANS, CHOPPED   ✳ *(Makes 6 servings)*

1. Marinate the seitan in the soy sauce and lime juice.
2. In a medium wok or skillet, sauté the lemongrass and lime leaves, if available, along with the ginger and garlic in 1/3 cup of stock for 3–5 minutes.
3. Add the onion and half the seitan marinade. When the onion is soft add the carrots, cauliflower, and broccoli stems with the rest of the stock.
4. After 5 minutes add the remaining vegetables, sauté them until they're tender, then add the seitan and its marinade and cook another few minutes. Pick out the lemongrass and lime leaves before serving.

Seitan Pepper Steak

When I was growing up, pepper steak was my father's favorite meal to prepare. I wanted to design a vegan version with a similar look and feel.

1 TABLESPOON OLIVE OIL

2 ONIONS, CUT IN RINGS

2 CLOVES GARLIC, MINCED

1 TABLESPOON GRATED GINGER

2 GREEN BELL PEPPERS, CUT IN STRIPS

2 RED BELL PEPPERS, CUT IN STRIPS

1 RECIPE SEITAN (PAGE **127**)

3 TABLESPOONS SOY SAUCE

1 TEASPOON TOASTED SESAME OIL   ✳ *(Makes 4 servings)*

1. Heat the olive oil in a medium wok or saucepan.
2. Add the onions, garlic, and ginger and cook for 5–10 minutes, until the onions are soft.
3. Add the bell peppers, seitan, and soy sauce, and cook another 5–10 minutes.
4. Add the toasted sesame oil and serve.

5

Side
Dishes

Vegetables

Grain and Bean Dishes

Eggplant Fillets

Crispy on the outside, tender on the inside, these cutlets go well with Spanakopita (page 98) or Greek Lasagna (page 80).

1 EGGPLANT, CUT IN **1/4**-INCH-THICK SLICES

3–4 TABLESPOONS OLIVE OIL

1/2 TEASPOON DRIED DILL

1/2 TEASPOON SEA SALT

1 TABLESPOON LEMON JUICE   ✳ *(Makes 6 servings)*

1. Preheat the oven to 375 degrees.
2. With a pastry brush, cover the bottom of a baking sheet with olive oil.
3. Spread the eggplant slices along the bottom of the pan. Mix the remaining ingredients and brush the top of the eggplant slices.
4. Bake for 10–15 minutes, until the eggplant is tender.

Roasted Veggies

This technique brings out the veggies' flavor to the fullest. My favorite pieces are the onion, fennel, and parsnips. Choose your favorites from the following veggies and prepare a total of about 3 pounds combined weight.

RED OR YUKON GOLD POTATOES, NOT PEELED AND CHOPPED

CARROTS, SLICED

PARSNIPS, SLICED

FENNEL BULB, CHOPPED

RED OR YELLOW ONION, CUT IN RINGS

RED OR GREEN BELL PEPPERS, CUT IN STRIPS

WATER TO COVER THE ABOVE VEGGIES

1/4 CUP CHOPPED FRESH BASIL

2 TABLESPOONS OLIVE OIL

1 TEASPOON SEA SALT

1/2 TEASPOON BLACK PEPPER   ✳ *(Makes 6 servings)*

1. Preheat the oven to 400 degrees.
2. Boil water in a medium saucepan. Cook the potatoes for 3 minutes, then add the carrots and parsnips and boil another 2 minutes. Drain.
3. In a large separate bowl, combine the basil, olive oil, sea salt, and black pepper.
4. Add all the vegetables and toss them until they're coated.
5. Spread the vegetables on a baking sheet and cook them on the top rack of the oven for 15–20 minutes, until they start to brown.

Szechuan Eggplant

Nothing holds flavor as fully as eggplant. Here it soaks up spicy Chinese seasonings.

1 EGGPLANT, CHOPPED IN BITE-SIZED PIECES

1 ONION, CHOPPED

2 CLOVES GARLIC, MINCED

1 TABLESPOON GRATED GINGER

1 TABLESPOON OLIVE OIL

2 TABLESPOONS SOY SAUCE

1 TABLESPOON RICE VINEGAR

1/2 TEASPOON HONEY OR RAW SUGAR

1 TEASPOON TOASTED SESAME OIL

CHILE OIL TO TASTE   ✻ *(Makes 4 servings)*

1. Sauté the eggplant, onion, garlic, and ginger in olive oil for 10–15 minutes, until the eggplant is soft.
2. Add the other ingredients and cook another five minutes.

Cajun Greens

I like to cook these particular greens until they're very, very soft, like traditional Southern fare.

1 ONION, CHOPPED

2 CLOVES GARLIC, MINCED

1 TOMATO, CHOPPED

1–2 TABLESPOONS OLIVE OIL

1 BUNCH CHARD, CHOPPED

1 BUNCH SPINACH, CLEANED AND TRIMMED

1 BUNCH COLLARD GREENS, CHOPPED

1 BUNCH KALE OR MUSTARD, CHOPPED

1 TEASPOON SEA SALT

3 TABLESPOONS VEGAN WORCESTERSHIRE (PAGE **178**)

TABASCO TO TASTE

✳ *(Makes 6 servings)*

1. In a medium saucepan, sauté the onion, garlic, and tomato in olive oil until the onion is soft.
2. Add the remaining ingredients and cook, covered, for 15–20 minutes, until the greens are soft.

Collard Greens
with Ginger and Tomato

Here collard greens are seasoned with ingredients common in East African cuisine.

1/2 ONION, CHOPPED

1 TABLESPOON GRATED GINGER

1 TEASPOON GROUND CUMIN

1/2 TEASPOON GROUND CORIANDER

PINCH GROUND CINNAMON

SEA SALT TO TASTE

1 TABLESPOON OLIVE OIL

1 TOMATO, CHOPPED

1 BUNCH COLLARD GREENS, CLEANED AND CHOPPED,
WITH THE STEMS REMOVED   ✳ *(Makes 4 servings)*

1. In a medium saucepan, sauté the onion, ginger, spices, and sea salt in olive oil until the onion is soft.
2. Add the tomato and cook another 5 minutes.
3. Add the collard greens and cook 10–15 minutes, until they're soft. Serve hot.

Italian Greens

Greens with basil and garlic go well with any lasagna.

3 CLOVES GARLIC, MINCED

1 TABLESPOON OLIVE OIL

1 TEASPOON SEA SALT

1/2 TEASPOON BLACK PEPPER

1 BUNCH COLLARD GREENS, CLEANED AND CHOPPED

1 BUNCH SPINACH, CLEANED AND TRIMMED

1 BUNCH MUSTARD GREENS, CHOPPED

1 BUNCH CHARD, CHOPPED

1 BUNCH KALE, CHOPPED

1 CUP FRESH BASIL LEAVES   ✳ *(Makes 4–6 servings)*

1. Sauté the garlic in olive oil in a medium saucepan.
2. Add the sea salt and black pepper, then the greens and basil, a little at a time, stirring often until they're all cooked.

Greek Potatoes

Lemony potatoes, prepared with garlic and Greek seasonings.

2 QUARTS WATER

6–8 MEDIUM RED POTATOES, NOT PEELED, CHOPPED

2 CLOVES GARLIC, MINCED

1 TABLESPOON OLIVE OIL

2 TABLESPOONS FRESH MINT

2 TABLESPOON FRESH DILL

1–2 TABLESPOONS LEMON JUICE

1 TEASPOON SEA SALT

1/2 TEASPOON BLACK PEPPER ✻ *(Makes 6 servings)*

1. Boil water in a medium saucepan and cook the potatoes until they're tender.
2. While the potatoes are cooking, sauté the garlic in olive oil in a small saucepan. Remove them from the heat and mix in the mint, dill, lemon juice, sea salt, and black pepper.
3. Toss the onion, garlic, and seasonings with the drained potatoes when they're ready.

Potatoes with Chiles

Serve these potatoes with salsa, or any south-of-the-border-style stew.

2 QUARTS WATER

6–8 YUKON GOLD, RED, OR YELLOW FINN POTATOES, NOT PEELED, CHOPPED

2 TABLESPOONS CHOPPED CILANTRO

1 TEASPOON SEA SALT

3 TABLESPOONS MILD GREEN CHILES, DICED (CANNED OR FRESH)   ✳ *(Makes 6 servings)*

1. Boil water in a medium saucepan and cook the potatoes until they're soft, about 10 minutes.
2. Drain and mix with the remaining ingredients.

Roasted Potatoes

Try these potatoes with Bean and Basil Burgers (page 122).

2 QUARTS WATER

2 POUNDS RED, YELLOW FINN, OR YUKON GOLD POTATOES,
NOT PEELED, CHOPPED

2 TABLESPOONS OLIVE OIL

1/2 TEASPOON SEA SALT

2 TABLESPOONS CHOPPED FRESH DILL

1/2 TEASPOON BLACK PEPPER   ✳ *(Makes 6 servings)*

1. Preheat the oven to 400 degrees.
2. In a medium saucepan, boil water and cook the potatoes for 5 minutes, then drain them and mix them with the other ingredients.
3. Spread them on a baking tray and roast them for about 20 minutes, until they start to brown.

Squash with Herbs

This is sweet and creamy and hits the same spot as mashed potatoes. Use this as a side dish with pasta or a casserole.

2 ACORN SQUASH

WATER FOR BAKING

2 TABLESPOONS CHOPPED FRESH BASIL

2 TABLESPOONS CHOPPED FRESH PARSLEY

1–2 TABLESPOONS LEMON JUICE

1 TEASPOON SEA SALT

BLACK PEPPER TO TASTE   ✳ *(Makes 4 servings)*

1. Preheat the oven to 400 degrees.
2. Cut the squash in half and scoop out the seeds. Cook the squash face down on a baking pan with 1/2 inch of water covering the bottom of the pan. Bake the squash for about an hour, until it's soft.
3. When the squash is cool enough to handle, scoop out the insides and mix it with the remaining ingredients.

Dried Tomato-Herb Bread

Basil, olives, and dried tomato in fresh, warm bread. Serve with pasta.

HANDFUL DRIED TOMATOES, SOFTENED IN BOILING WATER FOR A MINUTE OR TWO

1 CUP FRESH BASIL LEAVES

12–15 PITTED CALAMATA OLIVES

2 TABLESPOONS OLIVE OIL

1/2 TEASPOON SEA SALT

1/4 TEASPOON BLACK PEPPER

1 LOAF OF WONDERFUL, HARD-CRUSTED BREAD   ✳ *(Makes 4 servings)*

1. Preheat the oven to 350 degrees.
2. Purée all the ingredients except the bread in a food processor.
3. Slice the bread open lengthwise and spread it with the herb mixture.
4. Close the bread and wrap it in foil, and bake the bread for 10 minutes.

Gingered Yams

My Brazilian friend taught me to eat yams with curry powder. The ginger and lime juice seemed like natural additions.

3 YAMS

1 TEASPOON GRATED GINGER

1 TABLESPOON LIME JUICE

SEA SALT TO TASTE

1/2 TEASPOON CURRY POWDER   ✳ (Makes 4 servings)

1. Preheat the oven to 400 degrees.
2. Bake the yams for 1 to 1 1/2 hours, until they're soft.
3. When they're cool enough to handle, remove the skins and mash the flesh with the remaining ingredients.

Barley with Almonds

This barley pilaf goes well with Afghan Stew (page 120).

2 CUPS STOCK OR WATER

1 CUP PEARLED BARLEY

2 TABLESPOONS CHOPPED PARSLEY

1 TEASPOON SEA SALT

PINCH BLACK PEPPER

1/4 CUP SLIVERED ALMONDS   ✳ *(Makes 4 servings)*

1. Boil the stock or water in a small saucepan, then add all the ingredients except the almonds. Simmer until all the liquid is absorbed, about 20 minutes.
2. Mix in the almonds and serve.

Bulgur Pilaf

A nutty, cracked wheat pilaf.

2 CUPS BULGUR WHEAT

3 CUPS BOILING WATER

1/2 ONION, CHOPPED

1 CLOVE GARLIC, MINCED

1 TABLESPOON CHOPPED PARSLEY

1 TABLESPOON OLIVE OIL

1/4 CUP SUNFLOWER SEEDS

3/4 TEASPOON SEA SALT

✳ *(Makes 4 servings)*

1. Soak the bulgur in the water for 10 minutes.
2. Meanwhile, sauté the onion, garlic, and parsley in olive oil in a small skillet for 5 minutes.
3. Add the sunflower seeds and sea salt and mix all the ingredients together.

Polenta with Fresh Herbs

There is a common misconception that polenta is difficult to prepare. It's really not. It's also quite inexpensive and versatile, and you can add almost anything to it. Serve it with a stew on top, or cut slices and pan fry or broil them.

3 CUPS WATER

1 TABLESPOON OLIVE OIL

1 TEASPOON SEA SALT

1 CUP POLENTA

2 TABLESPOONS CHOPPED FRESH BASIL

2 TABLESPOONS CHOPPED FRESH PARSLEY   ✳ (Makes 4–6 serv-

1. In a medium saucepan, heat the water with the olive oil and sea salt.
2. When the water boils reduce the heat and drizzle in the polenta, stirring constantly, until it thickens. (It will thicken on the bottom before the top. Keep stirring until it's thick all the way through.)
3. Add the herbs and mix, then transfer it to a casserole pan to set.

Polenta with Chiles

Cook the polenta as described on page 154; when it thickens, add the following:

3 ANCHO CHILES, SOAKED IN WATER, DRAINED AND MINCED

2 TABLESPOONS DICED GREEN CHILES

1 TABLESPOON CHOPPED CILANTRO ❊ *(Makes 4 servings)*

Polenta with Olives and Dried Tomatoes

Cook the polenta as described on page 154; when it thickens, add the following:

10–12 PITTED CALAMATA OLIVES, SLICED

8–10 DRIED TOMATOES, BOILED FOR A MINUTE, THEN SLICED

2 TABLESPOONS CHOPPED FRESH BASIL ❊ *(Makes 4 servings)*

Kasha Varnishkes

This was one of my favorite foods when I was a child.

1/2 ONION, CHOPPED

6–8 MUSHROOMS, SLICED

1 TABLESPOON OLIVE OIL

1 CUP BUCKWHEAT GROATS

2 CUPS STOCK OR WATER

1 TEASPOON CHOPPED FRESH PARSLEY

1/2 CUP BOWTIE PASTA

1 TEASPOON SEA SALT   ✳ *(Makes 4 servings)*

1. In a small saucepan, sauté the onion and mushrooms in olive oil for about 5 minutes. Add the buckwheat, stir, and cook another 2 minutes.
2. Add the stock or water, bring it to a boil, then add the remaining ingredients and cook about 20 minutes, until the liquid is absorbed.

Curried Millet

Millet is a fluffy, healthy grain.

2 CUPS STOCK OR WATER

1 CUP MILLET

2 TABLESPOONS SESAME SEEDS

2 TABLESPOONS RAW SUNFLOWER SEEDS

1 TEASPOON CURRY POWDER

1 TEASPOON GRATED GINGER

1 TEASPOON SEA SALT   ✳ *(Makes 4 servings)*

1. Boil the stock or water in a small saucepan.
2. Add all the ingredients and simmer for about 20 minutes, until all the liquid is absorbed.

Basmati Pilaf

The fragrance of basmati rice makes this dish an excellent side for Afghan or East Indian curries.

2 CUPS WATER

1 CUP BROWN BASMATI RICE

SMALL HANDFUL DRIED CURRANTS

HANDFUL SLICED ALMONDS

1 TABLESPOON CHOPPED FRESH PARSLEY

1 TEASPOON SEA SALT   ✳ *(Makes 4 servings)*

1. Boil the water in a small saucepan and add the rice.
2. Add the remaining ingredients and cook on low heat until all the liquid is absorbed, about 30–40 minutes.

Wild Rice with Mushrooms

This is a satisfying, earthy side dish. Try it with Sesame Baked Tofu (page 100), or Squash Ratatouille (page 117).

3 1/2 CUPS WATER, DIVIDED

1/2 CUP WILD RICE

1 CUP BROWN RICE

1/2 ONION, CHOPPED

2 CLOVES GARLIC, MINCED

1/2 POUND BUTTON MUSHROOMS, QUARTERED

1 TABLESPOON CHOPPED FRESH PARSLEY

1 TABLESPOON OLIVE OIL

1 TEASPOON SEA SALT   ✳ *(Makes 4 servings)*

1. In a small saucepan, boil 1 1/2 cups water, then add the wild rice and reduce the heat.
2. In another small saucepan, boil the remaining 2 cups water, then add the brown rice and reduce the heat.
3. Sauté the onion, garlic, mushrooms, and parsley in olive oil with the sea salt for 10 minutes.
4. When both pots of rice have absorbed their water, mix all the ingredients together.

Fried Rice

This is the first meal I ever learned to cook. It works as a side dish, or as a main dish if you add seitan or tofu.

1 CUP BROWN RICE

1 ONION, CHOPPED

1 TEASPOON GRATED GINGER

1–2 TABLESPOONS OLIVE OIL

1 CUP BROCCOLI FLORETS

1 RED BELL PEPPER, DICED

2 CUPS STOCK OR WATER

2–3 TABLESPOONS SOY SAUCE ❊ *(Makes 6 servings)*

1. In a medium saucepan, sauté the rice, onion, and ginger in olive oil until the onion is soft, then add the broccoli and red bell pepper and cook another 5–10 minutes.
2. Add the remaining ingredients, bring the liquid to a boil, then cover the pan. Reduce the heat and simmer until the liquid is absorbed. Don't stir it until the rice is done.

Spanish Rice

Serve this as a side with Spanish Veggie Stew (page 114), or steamed veggies with Romesco Sauce (page 170).

2 CUPS VEGGIE STOCK OR WATER

1 CUP BROWN RICE

1 TOMATO, CHOPPED

1/2–1 TEASPOON SEA SALT

1 TEASPOON PAPRIKA

1/2 TEASPOON DRIED OREGANO

CAYENNE TO TASTE

✳ *(Makes 6 servings)*

1. Boil the stock or water in a small saucepan.
2. Add the remaining ingredients and cook, covered, for 30–40 minutes, until the liquid is absorbed.

Pulao

Rice and peas, East Indian style.

2 CUPS STOCK OR WATER

1 CUP BROWN BASMATI RICE

1/2 CUP FROZEN PEAS

1 TABLESPOON GRATED GINGER

1 TEASPOON GROUND CUMIN

1/2 TEASPOON GROUND CORIANDER

1/2 TEASPOON GROUND TURMERIC

1/2 TEASPOON GROUND CARDAMOM

1 TEASPOON SEA SALT   ✳ *(Makes 6 servings)*

1. Boil the stock or water in a small saucepan. Add all the ingredients and bring back to a boil.
2. Reduce the heat and cook until all the liquid is absorbed, about 40 minutes. Don't stir until the pulao is done.

Orzo Pilaf

I've heard it called, "rice under a microscope." Orzo is a pasta that looks like big grains of rice. This pilaf makes a good base for stews, especially Mediterranean ones.

2 QUARTS WATER

1/2 POUND ORZO PASTA

1 ONION, CHOPPED

2 CLOVES GARLIC, MINCED

1 TABLESPOON CHOPPED PARSLEY

1 TABLESPOON CHOPPED FRESH DILL

1 TABLESPOON CHOPPED FRESH MINT

1 TABLESPOON OLIVE OIL

1/2 TEASPOON SEA SALT

BLACK PEPPER TO TASTE

1–2 TABLESPOONS LEMON JUICE   ✳ *(Makes 4 servings)*

1. Boil water in a medium saucepan and add the orzo. Stir it often. (It is more prone to stick than other pastas because the pieces are so small.) Cook the pasta for 5 minutes, then drain it.
2. In a small saucepan, sauté the onion, garlic, parsley, dill, and mint in the olive oil.
3. Drain the pasta, mix it with the other ingredients, and serve.

Butterflies with Basil

Use this as a side dish for Seitan Cacciatore (page 131) or Squash Ratatouille (page 117).

---

1 POUND BUTTERFLY PASTA (ALSO KNOWN AS BOWTIES, OR FARFALLE)

WATER TO COVER

2 CLOVES GARLIC, MINCED

1 TABLESPOON OLIVE OIL

1 TEASPOON BALSAMIC VINEGAR

1/2 CUP CHOPPED FRESH BASIL

1 TEASPOON SEA SALT

BLACK PEPPER TO TASTE   ✳ *(Makes 4 servings)*

---

1. Cook the pasta in a medium saucepan for 10–12 minutes, then drain it.
2. In the meantime, sauté the garlic in olive oil for 1–2 minutes.
3. Mix all the ingredients together.

Marinated Black-Eyed Peas

Black-eyed peas are the most flavorful bean I know. The vinegar in this recipe complements their sweetness. Mix all the ingredients together. Serve hot or cold.

2 CUPS COOKED BLACK-EYED PEAS

1 ZUCCHINI OR GREEN BELL PEPPER, MINCED

1/2 RED ONION, DICED

3 TABLESPOONS RED WINE VINEGAR

1 TABLESPOON OLIVE OIL

1 TABLESPOON CHOPPED PARSLEY

1/2 TEASPOON SEA SALT

BLACK PEPPER TO TASTE

✳ *(Makes 4 servings)*

Black-Eyed Pea Dahl

Use it as a sauce on Spring Veggie Curry (page 86), or spoon it like a soup.

8 CUPS WATER

2 CUPS BLACK-EYED PEAS

1 TABLESPOON GRATED GINGER

2 CLOVES GARLIC, MINCED

2 TEASPOONS GROUND CUMIN

1 TEASPOON GROUND CORIANDER

1 TEASPOON GROUND TURMERIC

1/2 TEASPOON GROUND CARDAMOM

1 TEASPOON SEA SALT

CAYENNE TO TASTE   ❊ *(Makes 6 servings)*

1. Bring the water to a boil in a medium saucepan.
2. Add the remaining ingredients and cook for about an hour, until the black-eyed peas are soft.

6
Sauces, Marinades, and Condiments

Tomato Sauce

I have an Italian friend who regularly dreams about making tomato sauce. She tells me she's been known to wake up for a second in the middle of the night and say to her partner, "Could you go stir the sauce?"

1 ONION, CHOPPED

3 CLOVES GARLIC, MINCED

1 TABLESPOON OLIVE OIL

2 TABLESPOONS BASIL, FRESH OR DRIED

1 TEASPOON DRIED OREGANO

1 TEASPOON SEA SALT

1/2 TEASPOON BLACK PEPPER

1 CAN (28 OZ.) CRUSHED TOMATOES

1 CAN (6 OZ.) TOMATO PASTE

1 CUP WATER   ✳ *(Makes about 4 cups)*

1. In a medium saucepan, sauté the onion and garlic in olive oil. Add the seasonings.
2. Cook until the onion is translucent, then add the crushed tomatoes. Simmer for an hour and a half, stirring regularly. (If you use fresh basil, you don't need to cook it as long, but the longer you cook it, the better it will be.)
3. Add the tomato paste and water, and simmer for another hour.

Romesco (Spanish Tomato) Sauce

12–15 HAZELNUTS, SKINS ON

6–8 PITTED GREEN OLIVES

4 MEDIUM TOMATOES

2 TABLESPOONS RED WINE VINEGAR

2 CLOVES GARLIC, FINELY MINCED

10 SPRIGS PARSLEY

1 TEASPOON SEA SALT

1/2 TEASPOON BLACK PEPPER

✳ *(Makes nearly 2 cups)*

1. Chop the hazelnuts and olives coarsely in a food processor or blender. Remove them and set them aside.
2. Purée the remaining ingredients in a food processor or blender, then mix them with the chopped hazelnuts and olives.

Pesto

Pesto freezes quite well, so make plenty when basil is in season and enjoy it all year. This is good on pasta or pizza. Purée all the ingredients in a food processor or blender.

3 CUPS FRESH BASIL LEAVES

2 CLOVES GARLIC

1 CUP WALNUTS

1/2 CUPS DRIED TOMATOES, BOILED FOR **1–2** MINUTES AND DRAINED

2 TABLESPOONS OLIVE OIL

1/2 CUP CHOPPED FRESH PARSLEY

1 TEASPOON SEA SALT

1/2 TEASPOON BLACK PEPPER   ✳ *(Makes 2 cups)*

Muffaletta Sauce

This is quite versatile: you can also use it as a dip or as a sauce for veggies. Mix all the ingredients in a food processor or blender.

1 CAN ARTICHOKE HEARTS, DRAINED

1 CLOVE GARLIC

8–10 PITTED CALAMATA OLIVES

8–10 DRIED TOMATOES, BOILED IN WATER FOR ABOUT A MINUTE AND DRAINED

1/4 CUP FRESH BASIL LEAVES

1 TABLESPOON OLIVE OIL

1 TEASPOON SEA SALT

BLACK PEPPER TO TASTE   ✳ *(Makes about 1 1/2 cups)*

Fennel Tapenade

A little bit goes a long way. A couple of kids I know insist they hate olives, but you can't keep them away from this sauce. Purée all the ingredients in a food processor or blender.

1/2 CUP PITTED CALAMATA OLIVES

1 SMALL FENNEL BULB (ABOUT 1/2 CUP)

1 SMALL CLOVE GARLIC, MINCED

1 TABLESPOON RED WINE VINEGAR

2 TABLESPOONS CHOPPED RED ONION

1–2 TABLESPOONS OLIVE OIL   ✳ *(Makes about 1 cup)*

Plum Sauce

Use this as a sweet and salty dip for eggrolls or potstickers. Whisk the ingredients together.

2 JARS PLUM BABY FOOD

2 TABLESPOONS SOY SAUCE

1 TEASPOON TOASTED SESAME OIL   ✳ *(Makes about 1 cup)*

Black Bean Sauce

This sauce is a little less salty than most commercial black bean sauces (believe it or not), but full of flavor. Salted, fermented black beans are available in Asian groceries. Purée in a processor or blender.

1 PACKAGE (8 OZ.) SALTED BLACK BEANS, CLEANED AND RINSED

2 CLOVES GARLIC, MINCED

2 TABLESPOONS GRATED GINGER

2 TABLESPOONS RICE VINEGAR

1 TABLESPOON TOASTED SESAME OIL

1 TABLESPOON BROWN RICE SYRUP

1 CUP WATER   ✳ *(Makes nearly 2 cups)*

Sesame Sauce

I developed this recipe while trying to duplicate the cold sesame noodles from my favorite Chinese restaurant. Blend the tahini with water
and add the remaining ingredients.

1 CUP TAHINI

1 1/2 CUPS WATER

3 TABLESPOONS SOY SAUCE

2 TABLESPOONS RICE VINEGAR

1 TABLESPOON TOASTED SESAME OIL

1 CLOVE GARLIC, MINCED

1 TABLESPOON GRATED GINGER   ✳ *(Makes 3 cups)*

Mole Sauce

This is a tasty sauce to use on enchiladas, or mix with beans. You can also toss veggies in it, then roast them. Mix in a processor.

1 TABLESPOON UNSWEETENED COCOA

1 TABLESPOON CHILI POWDER

PINCH GROUND CINNAMON

1/4 TEASPOON HONEY

1/2 CUP COMMERCIAL RED SALSA, OR RED CHILE SALSA (PAGE **180**)

1 TABLESPOON DICED GREEN CHILES,
FRESH OR CANNED

✳ (Makes about 1/2 cup)

Peanut Sauce

This sauce goes exceptionally well with rice noodles. Blend the peanut butter and water, and mix the remaining ingredients.

1 CUP PEANUT BUTTER, CRUNCHY OR SMOOTH

1 CUP WATER

3 TABLESPOONS SOY SAUCE

2 TABLESPOONS LIME JUICE

1 CLOVE GARLIC, MINCED

1 TABLESPOON GRATED GINGER

2 TABLESPOONS COCONUT MILK

✳ (Makes a little more than 2 cups)

Almond Orange Sauce

The orange juice gives this recipe a light, unusual flavor. Chop the almonds in a food processor. Mix in the remaining ingredients.

1/2 CUP ALMONDS, WITH SKINS ON

1 TEASPOON GRATED GINGER

1/2 CUP ORANGE JUICE

2 TABLESPOONS SOY SAUCE

1 TABLESPOON RICE VINEGAR

1/2 CUP WATER   ❋ *(Makes about 1 1/2 cups)*

Teriyaki Marinade

Combine all the ingredients. Marinate any veggies, tofu, or seitan in this sauce, then roast them on a greased baking sheet until they start to brown.

1 CUP SOY SAUCE

1/2 CUP RICE VINEGAR

1 TABLESPOON HONEY MIXED WITH **2** TABLESPOONS HOT WATER

1 CLOVE GARLIC, MINCED

1 TEASPOON GRATED GINGER   ❋ *(Makes about 1 1/2 cups)*

Vegan Worcestershire

This recipe works well in any Cajun-style recipe and is also a tasty marinade for roasted veggies, tofu, or seitan.

1 TEASPOON GRATED GINGER

1/2 CUP WATER

1/4 CUP SOY SAUCE

1 TABLESPOON TAMARIND CONCENTRATE

2 TABLESPOONS MOLASSES   ✳ *(Makes about a cup)*

1. In a small saucepan, boil the ginger in the water for 10 minutes.
2. Strain the ginger and mix the liquid with the remaining ingredients.

Tomatillo Salsa

You can also make this salsa with fresh tomatillos. For sweet and sour pineapple salsa, add 1/2 cup canned or fresh pineapple. Purée all the ingredients in a food processor or blender.

2 CUPS CANNED CRUSHED TOMATILLOS

1/2 CUP CANNED MILD GREEN CHILES, DRAINED

1 BUNCH CILANTRO, STEMS REMOVED

3 TABLESPOONS RED WINE VINEGAR

1 TEASPOON SEA SALT   ✳ *(Makes a little more than 2 cups)*

Red Chile Salsa

This is a rich, somewhat spicy sauce that works as well on enchiladas as it does with chips. For chipotle salsa, boil 2 dried chipotle with the ancho chiles, or add 2 canned chipotle when you purée everything. For habanero salsa, add two fresh habanero peppers.

6 ANCHO CHILES

3 MEDIUM TOMATOES

1/2 BUNCH CILANTRO

3 TABLESPOONS RED WINE VINEGAR

1 TEASPOON SEA SALT   ✳ *(Makes about a cup)*

1. Soak the chiles in boiling water to cover for 10 minutes. Drain them and remove the stems. Leave the seeds if you want a hotter salsa; remove them if you want it milder. Wear gloves when you take out the seeds or wash your hands right after you handle them.
2. Purée the chiles with the remaining ingredients in a food processor or blender.

Tamarind-Date Chutney

Tamarind brings a perfect balance of sweet and sour to this sauce. Serve this chutney with any curry.

1/2 CUP PITTED DATES

1 TABLESPOON GRATED GINGER

1 CUP WATER

1 TABLESPOON TAMARIND CONCENTRATE (AVAILABLE IN INDIAN GROCERIES OR NATURAL FOODS STORES)   ✻ *(Makes about 1 cup)*

1. In a small saucepan, cook the dates and ginger in the water over medium heat, stirring often, for 20–30 minutes, until the dates start to break down.
2. Add the tamarind.

Faux Cheese

Use this sauce on top of baked pasta dishes or enchiladas. If you haven't eaten cheese recently, this will taste a little like it. Either way, it works well with any red sauce or salsa, and tastes much better than it sounds.

1/2 CUP WHOLE WHEAT PASTRY FLOUR (OR WHATEVER FLOUR YOU HAVE ON HAND)

1/2 CUP NUTRITIONAL YEAST, PREFERABLY LARGE FLAKE

1 TABLESPOON OLIVE OIL

3 CUPS WATER

1 TEASPOON SEA SALT

1 TEASPOON MUSTARD   ✳ *(Makes about 4 cups)*

1. Cook the flour and nutritional yeast in olive oil over low heat for 2 minutes in a medium saucepan, stirring constantly.
2. Add the water and bring it all to a boil, whisking to make a smooth mixture.
3. Simmer until it thickens to the consistency of thick soup, or a smoothie, then remove it from the heat and add the sea salt and mustard. It will thicken a little if you let it cool, but if you stir it, you should still be able to pour it.

7
Salads and Dressings

Greens Salad with Additions

I'm an avid fan of salad mix, which has become widely available during the past few years. You can almost always find a packaged variety, and many supermarkets also sell mixed salad greens in bulk in their produce sections. Look for salad mix at farmers' markets, too. Prepared, prewashed salad mix has a much wider variety of greens than I would have access to if I shopped for the greens individually, and I've always dreaded the task of cleaning, drying, and shredding greens (though I deeply admire people who do it graciously). I start with mixed greens as a base, and I add chopped tomato, red bell pepper, and cucumber. Try croutons and tamari-roasted sunflower seeds (page 186) for garnish. See pages 209–210 for dressings.

Croutons

4 SLICES HEARTY WHOLE WHEAT BREAD (STALE BREAD WORKS FINE. THIS IS AN
EXCELLENT USE FOR IT.)

1–2 TABLESPOONS OLIVE OIL

1/2 TEASPOON SEA SALT

1 TEASPOON DRIED BASIL   ✳ (Makes enough for a large salad)

1. Cut the bread into bite-sized chunks a day ahead of time and let it sit out and dry.
2. Preheat the oven to 350 degrees.
3. Toss the dried bread in the olive oil, sea salt, and basil.
4. Bake on a cookie sheet at 375 degrees for about 30 minutes, until the croutons are browned but not burned.

Tamari-Roasted Sunflower Seeds

1 CUP RAW SUNFLOWER SEEDS

2–3 TABLESPOONS TAMARI OR SOY SAUCE

1. Preheat the oven to 375 degrees.
2. Toss the sunflower seeds in the soy sauce.
3. Bake on a cookie sheet for about 20 minutes.

Marinated Potato Salad

This almost traditional potato salad uses fresh dill for an extra dimension of flavor.

2 POUNDS RED POTATOES, UNPEELED, CHOPPED, AND BOILED
UNTIL THEY'RE TENDER

1 RED ONION, CHOPPED

3 TABLESPOONS CHOPPED FRESH DILL

4 PICKLES, CHOPPED IN BITE-SIZED PIECES

1 TABLESPOON PREPARED MUSTARD

1 TABLESPOON OLIVE OIL

2 TABLESPOONS RED WINE VINEGAR

1/2–1 TEASPOON SEA SALT

1/2 TEASPOON BLACK PEPPER   ✳ *(Makes 6 servings)*

1. Combine all the ingredients and mix well.
2. Let stand 1/2 hour before serving.

Green Bean and Almond Salad

Make this salad in the high summer, when green beans are at their peak.

1/2 POUND GREEN BEANS, TRIMMED AND HALVED CROSSWISE

WATER FOR BLANCHING

10–12 CHERRY TOMATOES, CUT IN QUARTERS

1/4 CUP SLIVERED ALMONDS

1–2 TABLESPOONS OLIVE OIL

2 TABLESPOONS RED WINE OR BALSAMIC VINEGAR

1 TEASPOON DRIED DILL

1/2–1 TEASPOON SEA SALT

BLACK PEPPER TO TASTE   ✳ *(Makes 4–6 servings)*

1. Blanch the green beans by dropping them in boiling water for 30 seconds, then draining them and rinsing them immediately with cold water.
2. Mix the green beans with the remaining ingredients.

Marinated Cucumber Salad

I make this salad when I crave something green and have only a dollar to spend. Mix all the ingredients and serve.

1 LARGE CUCUMBER, PEELED AND CHOPPED

1 TEASPOON DRIED DILL

2 TABLESPOONS RED WINE VINEGAR

1 TABLESPOON OLIVE OIL

1/2 TEASPOON SEA SALT

PINCH BLACK PEPPER   ✳ *(Makes 4 servings)*

Asian Cucumber Salad

Serve this as a fresh, raw vegetable complement to Yakisoba (page 74). Stir it all together.

1 CUCUMBER, PEELED AND SLICED

2 TABLESPOONS SOY SAUCE

1 TABLESPOON RICE VINEGAR

1 TEASPOON GRATED GINGER

1 TABLESPOON BLACK SESAME SEEDS

1/2 TEASPOON HONEY OR
PINCH RAW SUGAR   ✳ *(Makes 4 servings)*

Corn and Green Bean Salad

This is a colorful salad of marinated veggies accented with dried tomatoes and sunflower seeds.

8–10 DRIED TOMATOES

1 CUP FROZEN CORN

2 CUPS GREEN BEANS, TRIMMED AND HALVED

1/4 CUP RAW SUNFLOWER SEEDS

2 RIPE TOMATOES, CHOPPED

1/2 RED ONION, CHOPPED

2 TABLESPOONS CHOPPED FRESH BASIL

1 TEASPOON DRIED MARJORAM

1 TABLESPOON BALSAMIC VINEGAR

1 TABLESPOON OLIVE OIL

1 TEASPOON SEA SALT

BLACK PEPPER TO TASTE   ✳ *(Makes 4 servings)*

1. Rehydrate the dried tomatoes by soaking them in boiling water for
   1–2 minutes.
2. Drain, chop, and mix them with the remaining ingredients.

Kim Chee

Spicy Korean coleslaw.

1 CUP RICE VINEGAR

1 TEASPOON SEA SALT

1 TEASPOON RAW SUGAR

1 TABLESPOON CRUSHED RED PEPPER (MORE OR LESS, TO TASTE)

1 ONION, CUT IN RINGS

1 TABLESPOON GRATED GINGER

2 CLOVES GARLIC, MINCED

1 CUP WATER

1 SMALL HEAD NAPA CABBAGE

2 CARROTS, GRATED

1 MEDIUM DAIKON RADISH, GRATED   ✳ *(Makes 6 servings)*

1. Heat the rice vinegar, sea salt, sugar, and crushed red pepper in a small saucepan with the onion, ginger, garlic, and water for 5 minutes.
2. Pour the sauce over the remaining ingredients and mix well.
3. Store it in the refrigerator. For the first day mix it every few hours. It will be tasty after a day, but better if you leave it a few days longer.

Mexican Tomato Salad

This salad makes a good counterpoint for Mexican dishes full of beans, like Tamale Pie (page 94) or Enchilada Pie (page 96). Mix all the ingredients.

4 RIPE TOMATOES, CHOPPED

1 MEDIUM ZUCCHINI, CHOPPED

1 CUP FROZEN CORN

1/4 CUP CHOPPED ALMONDS, WITH SKINS

2 TABLESPOONS DICED GREEN CHILES, FRESH OR CANNED

1 TABLESPOON CHOPPED CILANTRO

2 TABLESPOONS RED WINE VINEGAR

1 TABLESPOON OLIVE OIL

1 TEASPOON CHILI POWDER

1/2 TEASPOON GROUND CUMIN

1/2 TEASPOON DRIED OREGANO

1/2–1 TEASPOON SEA SALT   ✳ *(Makes 6 servings)*

Spinach-Basil Pasta Salad

This is a colorful, summery salad. The fresh spinach makes it especially vibrant.

1 POUND PRETTY PASTA

WATER TO COVER

1 BUNCH FRESH SPINACH, CLEANED, WITH STEMS REMOVED

2 RIPE TOMATOES, CHOPPED

1/4 CUP CHOPPED BASIL LEAVES

1/4 CUP SLICED BLACK PITTED OLIVES

3 TABLESPOONS RED WINE OR BALSAMIC VINEGAR

1 TABLESPOON OLIVE OIL

1 TEASPOON SEA SALT

BLACK PEPPER TO TASTE   ✳ *(Makes 6 servings)*

1. Cook and drain the pasta, then cool it by running cold water through it in the colander.
2. Mix the pasta with the other ingredients.

Spinach-Poppyseed Pasta Salad

Chives, lemon, and poppy seeds make a bright dressing for spinach and pasta.

1 POUND COLORFUL PASTA

WATER TO COVER

1 BUNCH SPINACH, CLEANED, WITH STEMS REMOVED

2 TABLESPOONS CHOPPED FRESH CHIVES

3 TABLESPOONS POPPY SEEDS

2 TABLESPOONS LEMON JUICE

1–2 TABLESPOONS OLIVE OIL

1/2 RED ONION, CHOPPED

1 TEASPOON SEA SALT

BLACK PEPPER TO TASTE   ✳ *(Makes 6 servings)*

1. Cook the pasta, then drain it and cool it with cold water.
2. Mix the pasta with the other ingredients.

Szechuan Noodle Salad

This spicy Asian noodle salad is one of my family's favorites.

1 POUND CAPPELINI PASTA

WATER TO COVER

1 MEDIUM DAIKON RADISH, GRATED

2 CARROTS, GRATED

1 CUP SNOW PEAS, TRIMMED AND HALVED

3 TABLESPOONS SOY SAUCE

2 TABLESPOONS RICE VINEGAR

1 TEASPOON HONEY

1 TEASPOON TOASTED SESAME OIL

1 TEASPOON CHILI OIL (MORE OR LESS TO TASTE)

3 GREEN ONIONS, CHOPPED

2 TABLESPOONS BLACK SESAME SEEDS
(AVAILABLE IN ASIAN GROCERIES)   ✳ *(Makes 6 servings)*

1. Cook, drain, and cool the pasta.
2. Mix the pasta with all the ingredients except the green onions and sesame seeds.
3. Sprinkle these on top of the salad, and serve.

Cashew Arame Noodle Salad

Arame is a sea vegetable that looks like black noodles, and contrasts nicely with the white noodles in this recipe. You can buy arame in a natural foods store. I like to make this salad around Halloween because of the black and orange colors.

2–3 QUARTS WATER

1 POUND RICE NOODLES (USE THE THIN ONES FROM CHINA.)

1 PACKAGE (2–3 OZ.) ARAME

1/2 CUP SOY SAUCE

1/4 CUP RICE VINEGAR

1 TEASPOON HONEY, MIXED WITH 2 TABLESPOONS WATER

2 CARROTS, GRATED

1/2 ONION, CHOPPED

1 TABLESPOON GRATED GINGER

2 CLOVES GARLIC, MINCED

1 TEASPOON OLIVE OIL

1/2 CUP CASHEWS
(I PREFER DRY ROASTED AND SALTED.)   ✻ (Makes 6–8 servings)

1. Boil the water, then turn off the heat and soak the rice noodles for 10 minutes.
2. Soak the arame in warm water for 5–10 minutes.
3. Drain the rice noodles and cool them with water. Rice noodles hold more water than wheat noodles, so shake the strainer to shed the extra water.
4. Combine the soy sauce, rice vinegar, and honey.
5. Drain the arame and mix together everything except the cashews.
6. Serve topped with cashews.

Vietnamese Noodle Salad

Here rice noodles show off a refreshing sauce of basil, mint, and lime. The thin rice noodles from China work best for this recipe.

2–3 QUARTS WATER

1/2 POUND RICE NOODLES

1 RIPE TOMATO, CHOPPED

2 TABLESPOONS CHOPPED FRESH BASIL

2 TABLESPOONS CHOPPED FRESH MINT

3 TABLESPOONS SOY SAUCE

2 TABLESPOONS LIME JUICE

1 TEASPOON GRATED GINGER

ANY OR ALL OF THE FOLLOWING VEGGIES:

1 CUP FINELY CHOPPED BOK CHOY

1/2 CUP BEAN SPROUTS

2 CARROTS, GRATED

1/2 CUP SNOW PEAS, TRIMMED AND HALVED   ✳ *(Makes 6 servings)*

1. Boil the water, turn off the heat, and soak the rice noodles for about 10 minutes.
2. Drain, cool with water, drain again, then mix the noodles with the remaining ingredients.

Thai Noodle Salad

Rich peanut sauce goes perfectly with these light noodles and veggies.

2 QUARTS WATER

1/2 POUND RICE NOODLES (USE THE THIN ONES FROM CHINA.)

1/2 BATCH PEANUT SAUCE (PAGE **176**)

1 CUP SHREDDED RED CABBAGE

1 BUNCH GREEN ONIONS, CHOPPED

1/2 CUP CHOPPED PEANUTS,
ROASTED, SKINNED

✳ *(Makes 6 servings)*

1. Boil the water, then turn off the heat and soak the rice noodles for 10 minutes. Drain and rinse the noodles to cool them.
2. Toss the rice noodles with the peanut sauce, transfer them to a serving bowl, then sprinkle the veggies and peanuts on top.

Lebanese White Bean Salad

White beans with Mediterranean flavors and crunchy cucumber. Mix it all together.

2 CUPS COOKED WHITE BEANS

1 CUCUMBER, PEELED AND CHOPPED

1 RIPE TOMATO, CHOPPED

1 TABLESPOON CHOPPED FRESH DILL, OR 1 TEASPOON DRIED DILL

1 TABLESPOON CHOPPED FRESH MINT, OR 1 TEASPOON DRIED MINT

1 TEASPOON GROUND CUMIN

1 TABLESPOON OLIVE OIL

1–2 TABLESPOONS LEMON JUICE

1/2–1 TEASPOON SEA SALT

BLACK PEPPER TO TASTE
　　　　　　　　　　　　　　　　✳ *(Makes 4–6 servings)*

Curried Garbanzo Bean Salad

Gingery garbanzo beans with marinated tomatoes. Mix all the ingredients. You can substitute 1 tablespoon curry powder for the cumin, turmeric, cardamom, and coriander.

3 CUPS COOKED OR **2** CANS GARBANZO BEANS, DRAINED

3 MEDIUM TOMATOES, CHOPPED

1 TEASPOON GRATED GINGER

1 TABLESPOON LEMON JUICE

1 TABLESPOON OLIVE OIL (OPTIONAL)

1/2–1 TEASPOON SEA SALT

1 TABLESPOON CHOPPED FRESH MINT

1 TEASPOON GROUND CUMIN

1/2 TEASPOON GROUND TURMERIC

1/2 TEASPOON GROUND CARDAMOM

1/2 TEASPOON GROUND CORIANDER   ✳ *(Makes 6 servings)*

Black Bean and Corn Salad

This is a very simple, very special salad. Serve it with Tamales (page 90) or other Mexican fare. Mix it all.

2 CUPS COOKED BLACK BEANS

2 RIPE TOMATOES, CHOPPED

1 SMALL CAN DICED MILD GREEN CHILES, DRAINED

1/2 RED ONION, CHOPPED

1 RED BELL PEPPER, CUT IN STRIPS (OPTIONAL)

1 CUP FROZEN CORN

2 TABLESPOONS CHOPPED CILANTRO

2 TABLESPOONS LIME JUICE

1 TEASPOON CHILI POWDER

1/2 TEASPOON GROUND CUMIN

1/2 TEASPOON DRIED OREGANO

SEA SALT AND CAYENNE PEPPER TO TASTE   ✳ *(Makes 6 servings)*

Tabouli

This salad works well with Hummus (page 17), Babaganoush (page 22), and Stuffed Grape Leaves (page 36). Serve it all with pita bread. Mix it all together. Let it stand half an hour before serving.

1 CUP BULGUR WHEAT SOAKED IN 1 1/2 CUPS HOT WATER FOR 15 MINUTES

2 RIPE TOMATOES, CHOPPED

1 BUNCH PARSLEY, CHOPPED

1 TABLESPOON CHOPPED FRESH MINT

1 TABLESPOON RED WINE VINEGAR

1–2 TABLESPOONS OLIVE OIL

2–3 TABLESPOONS LEMON JUICE

1 TEASPOON SEA SALT

1/2 TEASPOON BLACK PEPPER

Wild Rice Salad with Dried Tomatoes

3 1/2 CUPS WATER, DIVIDED

1/2 CUP WILD RICE

1 CUP BROWN RICE

3 1/2 CUPS WATER, DIVIDED

1/2 CUP SLICED GREEN OLIVES

2 TABLESPOONS CHOPPED FRESH PARSLEY

2 TABLESPOONS RED WINE VINEGAR

1 TABLESPOON OLIVE OIL

1 TEASPOON MUSTARD

1/2 TEASPOON ANISE SEED

1 TEASPOON DRIED ROSEMARY LEAF

10–12 DRIED TOMATOES, SOAKED IN HOT WATER AND SLICED

1/4 CUP RAW SUNFLOWER SEEDS   ✳ *(Makes 4–6 servings)*

1. In a small saucepan, boil 1 1/2 cups water and add the wild rice.
2. Twenty minutes later start heating the remaining 2 cups water in a different pan, and add the brown rice when it boils. Simmer them both until all the liquid is absorbed.
3. In the meantime, mix together the remaining ingredients. When the two kinds of rice are ready, cool them by running cold water through them in a colander, then mix them with the remaining ingredients.

Spelt and Tomato Salad

Spelt berries are crunchy on the outside and soft on the inside. They do a wonderful job of carrying the flavor of the basil and balsamic vinegar. Spelt berries are a lot like wheat berries, but many people who are allergic to wheat aren't allergic to spelt. You can find spelt berries and spelt flour in natural foods stores.

2 CUPS WATER

1 CUP SPELT BERRIES

2 RIPE TOMATOES, CHOPPED

2 TABLESPOONS CHOPPED FRESH BASIL

2 TABLESPOONS BALSAMIC VINEGAR

1 TABLESPOON OLIVE OIL

1/2–1 TEASPOON SEA SALT   ✳ *(Makes 4–6 servings)*

1. Boil the water in a small saucepan, then add the spelt berries and cook them, covered, until the water is absorbed, about 30–40 minutes.
2. Rinse the cooked grain in a colander to cool it, then mix with the remaining ingredients.

Couscous Salad

Couscous is semolina pasta, a variety of wheat widely used in North Africa and southern France.

3 CUPS WATER

2 CUPS COUSCOUS

1 CUP FROZEN PEAS

1 CUP GRATED CARROTS

1/4 CUP CHOPPED FRESH PARSLEY

1/4 CUP CHOPPED OR SLIVERED ALMONDS

1 TEASPOON GROUND CUMIN

1 TEASPOON DRIED MINT

2–3 TABLESPOONS LEMON JUICE

2 TABLESPOONS OLIVE OIL

1 TEASPOON SEA SALT

1/2 TEASPOON BLACK PEPPER   ✳ *(Makes 6 servings)*

1. Boil the water and pour it over the couscous. Let it soak, covered, for 10–15 minutes, until the couscous absorbs the water.
2. Add the remaining ingredients and mix.

Greek Salad

I love pickled, salty foods. This salad is full of them, with fresh veggies to balance them. Mix it all together.

1 CUCUMBER, PEELED AND CHOPPED

1 RIPE TOMATO, CHOPPED

1 CARROT, CHOPPED

8–10 PEPPERONCINI (GREEK PICKLED PEPPERS)

12–15 CALAMATA OLIVES

8–10 ARTICHOKE HEARTS, QUARTERED

2–3 TABLESPOONS RED WINE VINEGAR

1–2 TABLESPOONS OLIVE OIL

1 TEASPOON DRIED DILL

1/2 TEASPOON DRIED OREGANO

SEA SALT AND BLACK PEPPER TO TASTE   ✳ *(Makes 6 servings)*

Antipasto Salad

Serve this Italian salad with pasta or lasagna. Mix it all together.

2 CUPS COOKED OR CANNED CHICKPEAS, DRAINED

8–10 CANNED ARTICHOKE HEARTS, DRAINED

12–15 CALAMATA OLIVES

8–10 PEPPERONCINI

1 JAR (8 OZ.) ROASTED RED PEPPERS, DRAINED, CUT IN STRIPS

2–3 TABLESPOONS RED WINE VINEGAR

1–2 TABLESPOONS OLIVE OIL

1 TEASPOON DRIED BASIL

1/2 TEASPOON DRIED OREGANO

1/2 TEASPOON DRIED MARJORAM

1/2 TEASPOON DRIED TARRAGON

SEA SALT AND BLACK PEPPER TO TASTE   ✳ *(Makes 6 servings)*

Mustard Vinaigrette Dressing for Green Salad

My personal favorite. Shake the dressing up before serving.

1/2 CUP RED WINE VINEGAR

1/4 CUP OLIVE OIL

1 TEASPOON DIJON OR POUPON MUSTARD

1/2 TEASPOON DRIED DILL

1/2 TEASPOON DRIED TARRAGON

1/2 TEASPOON DRIED BASIL

1/2–1 TEASPOON SEA SALT

1/2 TEASPOON BLACK PEPPER ✳ *(Makes 4–6 servings)*

Tomato-Basil Salad Dressing

A no-oil dressing that takes moments to prepare.

1 CUP TOMATO JUICE

10–12 FRESH BASIL LEAVES, MINCED

1 TABLESPOON BALSAMIC VINEGAR

Tahini Dressing

A rich salad dressing that works well on steamed veggies, too.

1/2 CUP TAHINI

1–2 TABLESPOONS LEMON JUICE

1 TEASPOON FRESH OR DRIED PARSLEY

1 CLOVE GARLIC, MINCED

1/2 TEASPOON SEA SALT

1 TABLESPOON OLIVE OIL

3/4 CUP WATER   ✳ *(Makes a bit more than 1 cup)*

1. Mix all of the ingredients except the water in a food processor or blender.
2. Slowly add the water, and mix until the dressing is well combined.

8
Desserts

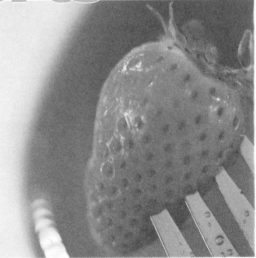

Date and Almond Rice Pudding

In my opinion it is particularly challenging to prepare fine, decadent desserts without eggs, butter, and refined sugar. Some people manage to do it; I would hesitate to count myself among them. I approach this challenge in two ways. First, I shy away from cake-like desserts, though I have found occasional vegan cake recipes that please me. Instead, I look for the types of desserts where the ingredients can stand on their own, like fruit salads and rice puddings. Secondly, I think of vegan desserts as appealing on their own terms, an alternative to the excessively sweet ones that are so familiar to us. This is a Middle Eastern dessert. The rose water gives it a lovely, exotic flavor. The rice milk is available in natural foods stores.

2 CUPS COOKED BROWN RICE

1/2 CUP CHOPPED PITTED DATES

1 CUP RICE MILK

1/4 CUP CHOPPED ALMONDS, WITH SKINS

2 TABLESPOONS RAW SUGAR OR 1 TABLESPOON HONEY

1/2 TEASPOON VANILLA

1/2 TEASPOON ROSE WATER   ✳ *(Makes 4–6 servings)*

1. Mix all the ingredients in a medium saucepan. Heat and stir.

Baklava

Baklava lends itself well to this vegan adaptation, since the original can be excessively sweet. You'll need an 11- by 17-inch baking sheet. A pastry brush will make your life simpler.

2 CUPS CHOPPED WALNUTS AND ALMONDS, MIXED

1 TEASPOON GROUND CINNAMON

2 CUPS HONEY

1/2 TEASPOON GROUND NUTMEG

1–2 CUPS CORN OIL

1 PACKAGE FILO DOUGH

✳ *(Makes 24 pieces)*

1. Preheat the oven to 350 degrees.
2. Mix the nuts with the cinnamon, honey, and nutmeg in a metal or Pyrex bowl.
3. Put the bowl in the oven, then shut off the heat.
4. With the pastry brush, paint a layer of oil on the baking pan. (If you don't have a pastry brush, spread the oil with a spoon. You'll end up using more oil.) Spread a sheet of filo on top, brush it with oil, and repeat with 11 more sheets.
5. Take the nuts and honey from the oven and spread the mixture as evenly and gently as possible over the filo.
6. Turn the oven on again to 375 degrees, then layer and brush the remaining filo.
7. Score the baklava by cutting through about half the layers. Don't cut down to the bottom or it will take forever to clean the pan. Cut in thirds vertically and in fourths horizontally, to make 12 rectangles. Then cut each rectangle on a diagonal, to make triangles.
8. Cover the pan with foil, making a tent so the foil doesn't touch the filo.
9. Bake for 20 minutes, covered, then uncover it and cook for another 10 minutes or so, until it's golden brown.

Hazelnut-Chocolate Chip Shortbread

Because shortbread uses no eggs, it lends itself well to a vegan inter-
pretation. You can't go wrong with chocolate and hazelnuts.

1 CUP (2 STICKS) MARGARINE

1 CUP HONEY

1 TEASPOON VANILLA

2 3/4 CUPS WHOLE WHEAT PASTRY FLOUR

1/2 TEASPOON SALT

1/2 CUP CHOPPED HAZELNUTS

1/2 CUP SUNSPIRE BRAND NONDAIRY,

BARLEY MALT-SWEETENED CHOCOLATE CHIPS ✳ *(Makes about 12 pieces)*

1. Preheat the oven to 350 degrees.
2. Mix the wet ingredients, then the dry ones in a separate bowl, then
   mix the two mixtures together.
3. Oil a 9- by 13-inch baking pan, then spread the batter and bake for
   about 30 minutes, until a knife stuck in the center comes out clean.

Almond-Rice Crispies

Not entirely unlike Rice Crispie treats. You can find the rice syrup in a natural foods store.

1 CUP COARSELY CHOPPED ALMONDS, WITH SKINS

2 CUPS CRISPY PUFFED RICE CEREAL

1 CUP RICE SYRUP

1 TEASPOON VANILLA   ✳ *(Makes 8 pieces)*

1. Mix the almonds and cereal.
2. Heat the vanilla and rice syrup in a small saucepan to a thin consistency, then mix them with the dry ingredients. Press the mixture into a pan to cool, then cut and serve.

Baked Apples

6 APPLES

1 CUP RAISINS

2 CUPS APPLE CRANBERRY
OR APPLE RASPBERRY JUICE   ✳ *(Makes 6 servings)*

1. Preheat the oven to 375 degrees.
2. Core the apples and stuff the centers with raisins.
3. Baste them with juice and bake them in a casserole pan or on a baking pan for about an hour.

Cocoa Halvah

A dense, nutty confection.

1 CUP SESAME SEEDS

1/4 CUP TAHINI

2 TABLESPOONS RICE SYRUP

1 TEASPOON VANILLA

2 TABLESPOONS COCOA POWDER   ✳ *(Makes 6 servings)*

1. Grind the sesame seeds in a food processor until some of them are powdered, about 3–5 minutes.
2. Heat the remaining ingredients together gently in a small saucepan, stirring often.
3. Mix in the sesame seeds, then press the mixture into a small loaf pan (or whatever you have available) and cool it. Cut in bite-sized pieces and serve.

Index

BOOKS BY THE CROSSING PRESS